The Hulton G

19

Decades of the 20th Century
Décadas del siglo XX
Decadi del XX secolo

The Hulton Getty Picture Collection

1960s

Decades of the 20th Century
Décadas del siglo XX
Decadi del XX secolo

Nick Yapp

KÖNEMANN

The trilingual edition in English, French and German first published in 1998 by Könemann Verlagsgesellschaft mbH, Bonner Straße 126, D-50968 Köln

This book was produced by The Hulton Getty Picture Collection Limited,
Unique House, 21-31 Woodfield Road, London W9 2BA

For Könemann:
Managing editor: Sally Bald
Project editor: Susanne Hergarden

For Hulton Getty:
Art director: Michael Rand
Managing editor: Annabel Else
Picture research: Alex Linghorn
Proof reader: Elisabeth Ihre
Production: Robert Gray
Design: Ian Denning
Picture editor: Ali Khoja
Editor: James Hughes
Scanning: Austin Bryan
Special thanks: Leon Meyer, Téa Aganovic and Antonia Hille

Colour separation by R&B Creative Services Group

Spanish translation: Carmen Gómez Aragón for Locteam, Barcelona
Italian translation: Giulio Lupieri for Ready-made, Milan
Typsettings: Ready-made, Milan

Project editors: Anabel Martín Encinas, Alessandra Provenzano
Production: Mark Voges
Printed and bound: Star Standard Industries Ltd

ISBN 3-8290-6176-5
10 9 8 7 6 5 4 3 2 1

Frontispiece: Dr Timothy Leary and his wife Rosemary on their honeymoon at Laguna Beach, California, 12 February 1968. The image is one of great purity, but to many Leary was the evil advocate of LSD and Marijuana.

Frontispicio: El Dr. Timothy Leary y su esposa Rosemary durante su luna de miel en Laguna Beach, California, 12 de febrero de 1968. La imagen desprende pureza e inocencia, pero, para muchos, Leary era el abogado del diablo del LSD y la marihuana.

Frontespizio: Timothy Leary e sua moglie Rosemary durante la luna di miele a Laguna Beach, California, 12 febbraio 1968. Il dottor Leary fu negli anni Sessanta il "grande sacerdote" dell'Lsd e della marijuana.

Contents / Contenido / Sommario

Introduction

The Sixties saw good and evil harvests from the seeds sown in the previous decade. In South Africa, apartheid produced the Sharpeville massacre and the assassination of Verwoerd. Castro's revolution in Cuba produced the Bay of Pigs fiasco. JFK was inaugurated President in 1961 and in a short time redefined the aspirations of an increasingly politicized population. The momentum created by the civil rights movement swept through the United States in the Sixties. In the ensuing turmoil Martin Luther King was gunned down; there were race riots in LA, Chicago, New York and Cleveland; and Malcolm X and Black Power burst upon the scene.

In Britain, the golden days of Prime Minister "Supermac" Macmillan and his consumer-driven conservatism were abruptly brought to an end by the Profumo scandal. In China, Mao Zedong unleashed the Red Guard. In Africa, Ian Smith led his Rhodesian settlers in an ultimately hopeless attempt to hang on to white power. Nelson Mandela was jailed for life. Jomo Kenyatta led his people to independence. The Greeks threw out their king. Violent death was the fate of Che Guevara in Bolivia, Adolf Eichmann in Israel, and the defenceless villagers of My Lai in Vietnam. Marilyn Monroe overdosed. Elvis Presley overate.

In 1968 all hell broke loose. The Soviet empire was shaken but not thawed by the Prague Spring. Paris almost had yet another revolution. Bobby Kennedy was assassinated. Civil war broke out in Biafra. There were riots in Chicago at the Democrat Convention. Black athletes gave the Black Power salute at the Mexico Olympics. In Europe and the States, schools and colleges became centres of anarchy, liberalism, pop culture and an ill-defined 'Red menace'. The Beatles endlessly repeated that 'All You Need Is Love', but it wasn't enough. Flower Power may have been initially beautiful; eventually it was ineffective.

All was conflict and argument. There were those who wished to extend higher education to all and sundry, while others preached the doctrine of deschooling. Drugs were good, drugs were bad. The Bomb was 'the great deterrent' or the great monster. Some reckoned Kennedy had saved the world by not backing down in the Cuban Missile Crisis. Others believed Khrushchev had saved the world because he did back down.

Disasters struck everywhere. At Aberfan, Wales, a vast pile of mud and slag slithered down a hillside and killed 144 people, 141 of them children. Florence was flooded. The oil tanker *Torrey Canyon* ran aground off Land's End, to give the world a taste of pollution to come.

Skopje was wrecked by an earthquake in the Balkans. The Ronan Point tower block collapsed in London. The Apollo Mission ended in tragedy at Cape Canaveral.

But there were also successes. The jumbo jet was born. Concorde roared through its maiden flight. The *QE2* ocean liner kept alive dreams of a romantic seafaring past, and Sir Francis Chichester sailed alone around the world. Yuri Gagarin became the first man in space. James Bond became the last word in sexy sophistication. Rudolf Nureyev danced his way into Western hearts and found asylum there. Bob Dylan reckoned the answer to it all was 'Blowing in the Wind', but many women found a better answer in the Pill.

Introducción

En los años sesenta se recogieron buenas y malas cosechas de las semillas plantadas en la década anterior. En Sudáfrica, el *apartheid* llevó a la matanza de Sharpeville y al asesinato de Verwoerd. La revolución de Castro en Cuba acabó con el fiasco de la bahía de Cochinos. John Fitzgerald Kennedy fue investido presidente en 1961 y, en poco tiempo, dio un nuevo sentido a las aspiraciones de una población cada vez más politizada. El impulso suscitado por el movimiento en defensa de los derechos civiles se propagó por EE.UU. en la década de los años sesenta. En el consiguiente tumulto cayó asesinado Martin Luther King; hubo disturbios raciales en Los Ángeles, Chicago, Nueva York y Cleveland; Malcolm X y el Black Power saltaron a escena.

En el Reino Unido, los días de gloria del primer ministro "Supermac" Macmillan y su conservadurismo consumista fueron interrumpidos abruptamente por el escándalo Profumo. En China, Mao Tse-tung desencadenó a la Guardia Roja. En África, Ian Smith dirigió a sus colonos de Rhodesia en un último intento desesperado de mantener el poder blanco. Nelson Mandela fue condenado a cadena perpetua. Jomo Kenyatta condujo a su pueblo a la independencia. Los griegos expulsaron a su rey.

El Che Guevara tuvo una muerte violenta en Bolívia, al igual que Adolf Eichmann en Israel, y los indefensos ciudadanos de My Lai en Vietnam. Marilyn Monroe falleció de sobredosis. Elvis Presley padecía bulimia.

En 1968 el cielo se desplomó. El imperio soviético fue sacudido por la Primavera de Praga, aunque salió intacto. París estuvo a punto de vivir una segunda revolución. Bobby Kennedy murió asesinado. La guerra civil estalló en Biafra. Se produjeron disturbios durante la Convención demócrata de Chicago. Los atletas negros hicieron el saludo del Black Power en los Juegos Olímpicos de México. En Europa y EE.UU., las escuelas y universidades se convirtieron en los reinos de la anarquía, el liberalismo y la cultura pop, todo lo cual fue mal definido bajo el mismo nombre de "amenaza roja". Los Beatles no se cansaban de repetir "All You Need is Love" (lo único que necesitas es amor), pero nunca fue suficiente. El Flower Power, pletórico de belleza en sus comienzos, resultó ser al final totalmente ineficaz.

Todo fueron conflictos y polémicas. Había quien reivindicaba una educación superior al alcance de todos, mientras que otros predicaban la desescolarización. Las drogas resultaban beneficiosas para unos y perjudiciales para otros. La bomba atómica era "la fuerza disuasoria" o el peor de los monstruos. Algunos creían que Kennedy había salvado al mundo al no ceder durante la crisis de los misiles cubanos. Otros veían en Jruschov al salvador del planeta porque sí había retrocedido.

Los desastres azotaron al mundo entero. En Aberfan, Gales, una enorme masa de barro y escoria se precipitó por la ladera de una colina y mató a 144 personas, 141 de las cuales eran niños. Florencia se inundó.

El petrolero *Torrey Canyon* encalló cerca de Finisterre para que el mundo degustara una pequeña parte de la contaminación que llegaría más tarde.

Skopje quedó asolado por un terremoto en los Balcanes. La torre Ronan Point se derrumbó. La misión *Apollo* acabó en tragedia en Cabo Cañaveral.

Sin embargo, también se vivieron algunos éxitos. Nació el avión a reacción *Jumbo*. El *Concorde* efectuó su primer vuelo. El transatlántico *Queen Elizabeth II* mantuvo vivos los sueños de los viajes por mar que pertenecían al pasado, y sir Francis Chichester navegó en solitario alrededor del mundo. Yuri Gagarin fue el primer hombre que voló por el espacio. James Bond se convirtió en el no va más en la sofisticación sexy. Rudolf Nureyev llegó a penetrar con su danza en los corazones occidentales y éstos le ofrecieron asilo. Bob Dylan creía que la respuesta para todo estaba "Blowing in the Wind" (en el aire), pero muchas mujeres preferían la píldora.

Introduzione

Gli anni Sessanta videro i buoni e i cattivi frutti dei semi gettati nella decade precedente. In Sudafrica, l'apartheid produsse il massacro di Shaperville e l'assassinio di Verwoerd. La rivoluzione di Castro a Cuba produsse l'incidente della Baia dei Porci. John Fitzgerald Kennedy fu eletto presidente nel 1961 e ridefinì le aspirazioni di una popolazione sempre più politicizzata. Il movimento per i diritti civili si diffuse negli Stati Uniti in questa decade. Le tensioni e i conflitti sfociarono nell'assassinio di Martin Luther King e nelle rivolte razziali di Los Angeles, Chicago, New York e Cleveland, con l'entrata in scena di Malcolm X e del movimento delle Pantere Nere.

In Gran Bretagna lo scandalo Profumo mise bruscamente fine ai giorni felici del Primo ministro "Supermac" Macmillan e del suo governo conservatore e filo-consumistico. In Cina Mao Tse-tung sguinzagliò le Guardie rosse. In Africa, Ian Smith guidò i coloni rhodesiani in un ultimo disperato tentativo di conservare il potere bianco. Nelson Mandela venne condannato all'ergastolo. Jomo Kenyatta portò il suo paese all'indipendenza. I greci detronizzarono il loro sovrano. Che Guevara fu ucciso in Bolivia, Adolf Eichmann in Israele e gli indifesi contadini di My Lai in Vietnam. Marilyn Monroe morì per overdose. Elvis Presley di bulimia.

Nel 1968 iniziò una nuova era. L'impero sovietico fu scosso dalla Primavera di Praga. Parigi visse contemporaneamente quasi un'altra rivoluzione. Bob Kennedy fu assassinato. In Biafra esplose la guerra civile. A Chicago vi furono violenti scontri durante la Convenzione democratica. Gli atleti di colore fecero il saluto delle Pantere Nere ai giochi olimpici di Città del Messico. In Europa e negli Stati Uniti, scuole e college erano diventati centrali di diffusione dell'anarchia, della liberalizzazione dei costumi e della nuova cultura pop. I Beatles ripetevano senza fine *All you need is love*, ma certamente non poteva bastare. I Figli dei fiori e la cultura hippie, che all'inizio avevano sedotto tanti giovani, alla fine finirono col perdere ogni contatto con la realtà.

Tutto era pretesto per discussioni e conflitti. C'erano quelli che volevano estendere a tutti l'educazione superiore, e quelli che predicavano la descolarizzazione. Le droghe erano buone per alcuni e cattive per altri. La bomba atomica era "il grande deterrente" o il grande mostro. Alcuni ritenevano che Kennedy avesse salvato il mondo non cedendo a Castro durante la crisi della Baia dei Porci. Altri erano invece convinti che il merito fosse di Krusciov.

Le catastrofi naturali devastarono il pianeta. Ad Aberfan, in Galles, un enorme smottamento di fango uccise 144 persone, 141 dei quali erano bambini. Firenze fu allagata. La petroliera *Torrey Canyon* affondò a Land's End, in Inghilterra, quasi ad annunciare le maree nere dei decenni successivi.

Nei Balcani, Skopje fu devastata da un terremoto. A Londra crollò la torre Ronan Point. La missione Apollo si concluse in una tragedia a Cape Canaveral.

Ma ci furono anche lieti eventi. Nacque il Jumbo, primo aereo gigante, e il Concorde fece i primi voli di prova. La *Queen Elizabeth II* mantenne vivi i sogni delle romantiche crociere del passato e Sir Francis Chichester portò a termine il suo primo giro del mondo in solitaria. Yuri Gagarin diventò il primo uomo dell'era spaziale. James Bond diventò il simbolo del *sex appeal* maschile. A passi di danza, Rudpolf Nureyev conquistò i cuori degli occidentali e trovò asilo in Europa. Per Bob Dylan la risposta a tutto era *Blowing in the Wind*, ma molte donne trovarono una risposta migliore nella pillola.

1. Movers and shakers
Líderes y agitadores
Progressisti e agitatori

John Fitzgerald Kennedy, the 35th president of the United States, 31 May 1961. From his inauguration to his assassination, Kennedy led his country for just 1,037 days, but his impact on politics in the Sixties was immense.

John Fitzgerald Kennedy, 35° presidente de EE.UU., el 31 de mayo de 1961. Desde su investidura hasta su asesinato, Kennedy presidió el país durante sólo 1.037 días, pero ejerció una enorme influencia en la política de los años sesenta.

John Fitzgerald Kennedy, il trentacinquesimo presidente degli Stati Uniti, 31 maggio 1961. Dalla sua elezione al suo assassinio, Kennedy guidò il suo paese per 1037 giorni, ma il suo impatto sulla politica degli anni Sessanta fu enorme.

1. Movers and shakers
Líderes y agitadores
Progressisti e agitatori

Not since the 1840s or the 1920s had there been such tumultuous political upheavals throughout the world. The alphabet of instability began with Algeria and apartheid, went on to Biafra and the Berlin Wall, the Congo and Cuba, and worked its way right through to Vietnam. The dramas were tragic, exciting, uplifting, depressing, shocking and continuous.

At the beginning of the decade Eisenhower was still president of the USA and Churchill remained a senior statesman in Britain. By the time the Sixties whirled to their end, both were dead, Nixon had sweated his way into the White House, Ho Chi Minh had died, and de Gaulle was a spent force.

There were those who had their brief spell of fame and glory – Alexander Dubček, Che Guevara, Ian Smith. There were those who stayed the distance – Mao Zedong and President Tito looked set to last forever. And there were some names that were never out of the headlines. JFK was killed in 1963, his brother Bobby five years later. Chappaquiddick dented Edward Kennedy's career in July 1969, and four months later old Joe Kennedy died.

Nelson Mandela began his 26 years in prison in 1964. Two years later, the man who put him there, Hendrik Verwoerd was stabbed to death by a white extremist.

No se recordaban tantos y tan tumultuosos trastornos políticos en todo el mundo desde 1840 o 1920.

El alfabeto de la inestabilidad empezó con la A de Argelia y el *apartheid,* continuó con Biafra y el muro de Berlín, el Congo y Cuba, y acabó con la V de Vietnam. Los acontecimientos eran trágicos, excitantes, edificantes, deprimentes, asombrosos e interminables.

A principios de la década Eisenhower era aún presidente de EE.UU. y Churchill, un importante hombre de Estado en el Reino Unido. A finales de los años sesenta, ambos estaban muertos, Nixon se había abierto camino hacia la Casa Blanca, Ho Chi Minh también había fallecido y De Gaulle era una fuerza agotada.

Algunos, como Alexander Dubček, el Che Guevara o Ian Smith, vivieron breves momentos de gloria y celebridad. Otros, mantuvieron las distancias, como Mao Tse-tung y el presidente Tito, y parecía que iban a durar eternamente. Y hubo también ciertos nombres omnipresentes en los grandes titulares. JFK fue asesinado en 1963, y su hermano Bobby, cinco años más tarde. El accidente de Chappaquiddick arruinó la carrera de Edward Kennedy, en julio de 1969; cuatro meses después, murió el patriarca Joe Kennedy.

En 1964 Nelson Mandela empezó a cumplir su pena de 26 años de cárcel. Al cabo de dos años, el hombre que le había condenado, Hendrik Verwoerd, fue apuñalado a muerte por un extremista blanco.

Era dagli anni 1840 o 1920 che nel mondo non si verificavano tanti tumulti e sollevazioni. L'alfabeto dell'instabilità iniziava con Algeria e apartheid, per continuare con Biafra e Berlino (il Muro), Congo e Cuba, proseguendo fino alla lettera V come Vietnam. I drammi erano di volta in volta tragici, appassionanti, incoraggianti, demoralizzanti, ma soprattutto continui.

All'inizio della decade Eisenhower era ancora presidente degli Stati Uniti e Winston Churchill un importante uomo di stato in Gran Bretagna. Alla fine degli anni Sessanta, i due uomini erano morti. Nixon era salito alla Casa Bianca, Ho Chi Minh era scomparso e de Gaulle era al termine della sua carriera.

Alcuni, come Aleksander Dubček, Che Guevara o Ian Smith conobbero un breve momento di gloria. Altri, come Mao Tse-tung e il presidente Tito, sembravano intramontabili. John Fitzgerald Kennedy fu assassinato nel 1963, suo fratello Bobby cinque anni più tardi. Chappaquiddick rovinò la carriera di Edward Kennedy nel luglio del 1969 e quattro mesi dopo morì il vecchio Joe Kennedy.

Nelson Mandela iniziò i suoi 26 anni di detenzione nel 1964. Due anni più tardi, l'uomo che l'aveva condannato, Hendrik Verwoerd, fu pugnalato a morte da un estremista bianco.

A heated exchange during the Cold War. Vice-President Nixon of the United States gives the finger to the Soviet premier, Nikita Khrushchev, in the aftermath of the U2 spy plane crisis, 1960.

Acalorada entrevista durante la guerra fría. El vicepresidente de EE.UU., Nixon, apunta a Nikita Jruschov con un dedo amenazador tras la crisis de los aviones espías *U2*, en 1960.

Un appassionato scambio di opinioni durante la guerra fredda. Il presidente degli Stati Uniti Richard Nixon punta il dito contro il premier sovietico Nikita Krusciov dopo la crisi degli aerei spia U2, 1960.

A happier handshake. President John Kennedy and Khrushchev meet at the US Embassy in Vienna in June 1961. Their apparent friendship was totally false. Two months earlier, relations between the USA and the Soviet Union had been strained to the limit by the Bay of Pigs incident in Cuba.

Un saludo más cordial. Encuentro del presidente John Kennedy y Jruschov en la embajada de EE.UU. en Viena, junio de 1961. Su aparente amistad era completamente fingida. Dos meses antes, las relaciones entre EE.UU. y la URSS alcanzaron el momento de mayor tensión hasta entonces, a raíz del incidente de la bahía de Cochinos, en Cuba.

Una più cordiale stretta di mano. Il presidente John Kennedy e Krusciov davanti all'ambasciata americana di Vienna nel giugno 1961. La cordialità era però solo apparente. Due mesi dopo i rapporti tra gli Stati Uniti e l'Unione Sovietica si fecero di nuovo tesi con l'incidente della Baia dei Porci a Cuba.

The new attraction, 1961. Sightseers climb atop a tour bus to look over the newly built Berlin Wall. It stayed there for another 28 years.

La nueva atracción, 1961. Un grupo de turistas sube a lo alto de su autobús para mirar al otro lado del recién construido muro de Berlín. El muro seguiría allí durante 28 años.

La nuova attrazione, 1961. Alcuni curiosi si arrampicano sul tetto di un autobus per guardare al di là del Muro di Berlino, appena eretto. Il Muro resistette per altri 28 anni.

Hot and cold – hot. In the warm days of summer, Nikita Khrushchev and President Josip Tito of Yugoslavia relax together on the *Podgorka*, during a sight-seeing trip along the Istrian coast, 26 August 1963. It was another uneasy friendship.

¿Frío o caliente? Caliente. Nikita Jruschov y el presidente de Yugoslavia, Josip Tito, comparten la calma de un cálido día de verano en el *Podgorka*, durante una salida en barco a lo largo de la costa de Istria el 26 de agosto de 1963. Otra amistad algo tensa.

Caldo o freddo? Caldo. In una calda giornata d'estate Nikita Krusciov e il presidente della Jugoslavia Josip Tito si rilassano sulla *Podgorka* durante una crociera lungo le coste dell'Istria, 26 agosto 1963. Un'altra difficile amicizia.

Hot and cold – cold. Khrushchev and the president of Finland, Urho Kekkonen (left), meet dressed for a hunting trip in December 1963. Each was probably the other's preferred kill.

¿Frío o caliente? Frío. Jruschov y el presidente de Finlandia, Urho Kekkonen (izquierda), vestidos para salir de caza, diciembre de 1963. Probablemente, cada uno era la presa preferida del otro.

Caldo o freddo? Freddo. Krusciov e il presidente finlandese Urho Kekkonen (a sinistra) pronti a partire per una battuta di caccia nel dicembre 1963. Per ognuno di loro la preda più ambita sarebbe forse stata l'altro.

Khrushchev and Polish president Wladyslaw Gomulka in jovial mood at the United Nations, New York, 22 September 1960. Two weeks later, Khrushchev pounded his desk in rage at the UN, accused by a Philippine diplomat of depriving Poland and others of 'political and civil rights'.

Jruschov y el presidente polaco Wladyslaw Gomulka de buen homor en la sede de las Naciones Unidas, Nueva York, 22 de septiembre de 1960. Dos semanas después, Jruschov golpeó enfurecido su escaño en la ONU al ser acusado por un diplomático filipino de privar a Polonia y a otros países de sus “derechos políticos y civiles”.

Krusciov e il presidente polacco Wladyslaw Gomulka alle Nazioni Unite, New York 22 settembre 1960. Due settimane dopo Krusciov batté i pugni sul suo banco alle Nazioni Unite, accusato da un diplomatico filippino di privare la Polonia e altri paesi dei “diritti civili e politici”.

Khrushchev's successor, Leonid Brezhnev, meets Alexander Dubček of Czechoslovakia at the Bratislava summit, 7 August 1968. Two weeks later, Soviet tanks were crushing the Prague experiment in 'liberalization'.

Encuentro del sucesor de Jruschov, Leonid Brezhnev, con el checoslovaco Alexander Dubček durante la cumbre de Bratislava, el 7 de agosto de 1968. A las dos semanas, los carros soviéticos aplastaron el experimento "liberalizador" de Praga.

Il successore di Krusciov, Lleonid Breznev, incontra il cecoslovacco Alexander Dubček al summit di Bratislava, 7 agosto 1968. Due settimane dopo i carri armati russi soffocarono l'esperimento praghese di "liberalizzazione".

March 1962. Gary Powers, pilot of the U2 spy plane that crashed in the Soviet Union, gives evidence before a US Senate Armed Forces Committee, Washington DC.

Marzo de 1962. Gary Powers, piloto del avión espía *U2* que se estrelló en la Unión Soviética, testifica ante un comité de las fuerzas aéreas estadounidenses en el Senado, Washington D.C.

Marzo 1962. Gary Powers, pilota dell'aereo spia U2 che precipitò in Unione sovietica, testimonia al Senato durante l'inchiesta condotta da un Comitato dell'aviazione americana, Washington D.C.

The Cuban missiles on their way back to the Soviet Union. This picture was taken from a US reconnaissance aircraft, 12 November 1962. The missiles can be seen lashed to the deck of the cargo ship.

Los misiles cubanos regresan a la URSS. Esta fotografía se tomó desde un avión estadounidense de reconocimiento, el 12 de noviembre de 1962. En ella se ven los misiles amarrados en la cubierta del barco.

I missili cubani fanno ritorno in Unione sovietica. La fotografia è stata scattata da un aereo di ricognizione americano, il 12 novembre 1962. Sul ponte della nave si possono scorgere i missili.

In the year of his election victory, John Kennedy relaxes in his rocking chair. It brought him relief from frequent back pain.

John Kennedy descansa en su mecedora, en una fotografía del año de su victoria electoral. El balanceo le aliviaba sus frecuentes dolores de espalda.

L'anno in cui venne eletto alla Casa Bianca, John Kennedy si rilassa sulla sua sedia a dondolo, che arrecava sollievo ai suoi frequenti dolori di schiena.

Jacqueline Lee Bouvier, better known as Jackie Kennedy, 1961. She sometimes wearied of being one half of a couple known as 'Jack and Jackie'.

Jacqueline Lee Bouvier, más conocida como Jackie Kennedy, en 1961. A veces le pesaba ser la mitad de una pareja conocida como "Jack y Jackie".

Jacqueline Lee Bouvier, meglio nota come Jackie Kennedy, 1961, cui spesso stava stretto il ruolo della metà di una coppia soprannominata "Jack e Jackie".

The shots that shook the world, Dallas, 22 November 1963. The JFK motorcade sweeps past the grassy knoll and all hell breaks out.

Los disparos que estremecieron al mundo, Dallas, 22 de noviembre de 1963. La comitiva de JFK pasa ante un montículo de césped y luego se desencadenaría un infierno.

Lo sparo che scosse il mondo, Dallas, 22 novembre 1963. Il corteo presidenziale passa davanti a un'aiuola verde e poi esplode l'inferno.

Officially, this is the rifle with which Lee Harvey Oswald shot President Kennedy. The picture was taken in 1965, during the Warren Commission inquiry into the assassination.

Oficialmente, éste es el rifle que Lee Harvey Oswald utilizó para matar al presidente Kennedy. La fotografía se tomó en 1965, durante la investigación acerca del asesinato llevada a cabo por la comisión Warren.

Ufficialmente, questo è il fucile con cui Lee Harvey Oswald uccise il presidente Kennedy. La fotografia è stata scattata nel 1965, durante l'inchiesta della Commissione Warren.

Ninety-nine minutes after the shots were fired, Lyndon Johnson is sworn in as president of the United States on board *Air Force One*, 22 November 1963. On his right is Mrs Johnson, on his left, Jackie Kennedy.

Noventa y nueve minutos después del atentado, Lyndon Johnson prestó juramento como presidente de EE.UU. a bordo del avión *Air Force One,* 22 de noviembre de 1963. A su derecha, la señora Johnson y, a su izquierda, Jackie Kennedy.

Novantanove minuti dopo gli spari di Dallas, Lyndon Johnson presta il giuramento presidenziale a bordo dell'*Air Force One*, il 22 novembre 1963. Alla sua sinistra la signora Johnson, a destra Jackie Kennedy.

Jack Ruby kills Lee Harvey Oswald, 24 November 1963. The incident happened as Oswald was being led out of the basement of the Dallas municipal office, and was seen by millions on television.

El 24 de noviembre de 1963 Jack Ruby asesina a Harvey Oswald. El incidente ocurrió mientras conducían a Oswald desde los sótanos del ayuntamiento de Dallas, y lo vieron millones de personas por televisión.

Jack Ruby uccide Lee Harvey Oswald, 24 novembre 1963. L'incidente avvenne mentre Oswald veniva trasferito dal sottosuolo del tribunale e fu visto alla televisione da milioni di persone.

Ernesto Che Guevara, Argentinian revolutionary leader, 1965. Guevara helped Fidel Castro in his war to free Cuba. In the Sixties, his picture became an icon for the Left.

Ernesto Che Guevara, líder revolucionario argentino, en 1965. Guevara ayudó a Fidel Castro en su guerra para la liberación de Cuba. Su imagen se convirtió en el icono de la izquierda en los años sesenta.

Ernesto Che Guevara, leader rivoluzionario argentino, 1965. Il Che aiutò Fidel Castro nella sua guerra per liberare Cuba. Negli anni Sessanta il suo volto divenne un'icona della sinistra.

January 1962.
Prime Minister Fidel Castro 'at bat' to open a baseball tournament in Havana, Cuba.

Enero de 1962.
El primer ministro Fidel Castro inaugura, bate en mano, un torneo de béisbol en La Habana, Cuba.

Gennaio 1962. Il Primo ministro Fidel Castro nelle vesti del battitore alla cerimonia di apertura di un torneo di baseball all'Avana, Cuba.

Mao Zedong relaxes, 1963. His popularity in China waned in the early Sixties, after the comparative failure of the 'Great Leap Forward'. Three years later came the Cultural Revolution, and Mao was once more in firm control.

Un momento de descanso para Mao Tse-tung, 1963. Su popularidad disminuyó en China a principios de los años sesenta a causa del relativo fracaso del "Gran paso adelante". Tres años después nacería la revolución cultural y con ella Mao recuperó de nuevo el control del poder.

Mao Tse-tung si rilassa, 1963. All'inizio degli anni Sessanta, dopo il fallimento del "Grande balzo in avanti", la sua popolarità crollò. Tre anni dopo, con la Rivoluzione culturale, Mao riacquistò il controllo.

A chorus sing the praises of their beloved Mao during a break in the wheat harvest near Beijing, July 1967. No doubt *The Thoughts of Chairman Mao* were in the thoughts of every singer.

Un coro canta las alabanzas a su venerado Mao durante una pausa en la recolección de trigo cerca de Pekín, julio de 1967. No cabe duda de que todos los cantores tenían muy presentes *Los pensamientos del presidente Mao*.

Un coro canta le lodi dell'amato presidente Mao durante una pausa nella raccolta del grano nei pressi di Pechino, luglio 1967. I *Pensieri del presidente Mao* erano bene impressi nella mente di ogni cantante.

October 1967, and the Chinese Cultural Revolution is well under way. Members of the Provincial Revolution Committee paint anti-capitalist slogans on banners, as part of a drive to attack those in authority deemed to have capitalist leanings.

Octubre de 1967; la revolución cultural china está en todo su auge. Miembros de un comité revolucionario provincial pintan consignas anticapitalistas en unas pancartas como parte de una campaña de ataques contra ciertos dirigentes por sus supuestas inclinaciones capitalistas.

Ottobre 1967, in piena Rivoluzione culturale cinese. I membri del Comitato rivoluzionario provinciale dipingono slogan anticapitalisti su striscioni e cartelli nell'ambito di una campagna contro i dirigenti di partito filocapitalisti.

Holding copies of the famous *Little Red Book*, followers of Mao taunt members of the Chinese embassy staff in London, 1967.

Provistos de ejemplares del famoso *Libro rojo*, los seguidores de Mao ridiculizan a los miembros de la embajada china en Londres, 1967.

Con in mano il famoso *Libretto rosso*, i seguaci di Mao criticano i membri dell'ambasciata cinese a Londra, 1967.

Political campaigning, US style. Holding placards that read 'I like Dick' and 'Hump for Crump', Republican supporters from the Clothing Export Council back their nomination, Nixon, and show their opposition to Humphrey, in the 1968 presidential election.

Campaña política a la americana. Con pancartas como "Me gusta Dick" y "Abajo Hump", las seguidoras republicanas del consejo para la exportación de indumentaria apoyan la candidatura de Nixon y muestran su rechazo a Humphrey durante las elecciones presidenciales de 1968.

Campagna elettorale in puro stile americano. Con cartelli che dicono "Mi piace Dick", "Abbasso Hump", alcune elettrici repubblicane del Consorzio per l'esportazione dell'abbigliamento esprimono il loro sostegno a Nixon alle elezioni presidenziali del 1968.

On the trail to the White House, November 1968. Richard Milhous Nixon looks unnaturally confident in his bid to become president – Nixon's return to power was a close call.

Camino de la Casa Blanca, noviembre de 1968. Richard Milhous Nixon se muestra asombrosamente seguro de su triunfo electoral. Sin embargo, Nixon volvió al poder por los pelos.

In cammino verso la Casa Bianca, novembre 1968. Richard Milhous Nixon sembra straordinariamente sicuro di riuscire a diventare presidente. La sua fu però una vittoria di stretta misura.

New Delhi, April 1961. The Dalai Lama (left), leader of Tibet, meets Jawaharlal Nehru, prime minister of India. They were discussing the rehabilitation of Tibetans who had crossed the Indian border during the Sino-Tibetan crisis.

Nueva Delhi, abril de 1961. Encuentro del Dalai Lama (izquierda), guía espiritual del Tíbet, y Jawaharlal Nehru, primer ministro de India, para discutir la rehabilitación de los tibetanos que habían cruzado la frontera india durante la crisis sinotibetana.

Nuova Delhi, aprile 1961. Il Dalai Lama (a sinistra), leader del Tibet, incontra Jawalharlal Nehru, primo ministro indiano, per discutere dell'integrazione dei tibetani rifugiati in India durante la crisi sino-tibetana.

Members of the Gandhi dynasty of India, in the garden of their New Delhi home, 1967. (Left to right) Sanjay Gandhi, his mother Indira Gandhi (then prime minister of India), and his brother Rajiv.

Miembros de la dinastía Gandhi en el jardín de su casa en Nueva Delhi, 1967. (De izquierda a derecha) Sanjay Gandhi, su madre Indira Gandhi (entonces primera ministra de la India) y su hermano Rajiv.

I membri della dinastia indiana dei Gandhi nei giardini della loro residenza a Nuova Delhi, 1967. (Da sinistra a destra) Sanjay Gandhi, sua madre Indira Gandhi (allora primo ministro) e il fratrello Rajiv.

A brief happy moment in a year which was largely spent on the run from the authorities. Winnie and Nelson Mandela embrace, 1962.

Un breve instante de felicidad en un año dedicado, en su mayor parte, a huir de las autoridades. Abrazo de Winnie y Nelson Mandela, 1962.

Un breve attimo di felicità dopo un anno trascorso quasi interamente a sfuggire alle autorità. Winnie tra le braccia di Nelson Mandela, 1962.

Eminence Blanche: Dr Hendrik Verwoerd, prime minister of South Africa and high priest of the foul doctrine of apartheid, March 1961.

La eminencia blanca: El Dr. Hendrick Verwoerd, primer ministro de Sudáfrica y ferviente defensor de las doctrinas xenófobas del *apartheid*, marzo de 1961.

L'eminenza bianca: il dottor Hendrik Verwoerd, primo ministro del Sudafrica e fervente sostenitore dell'immonda dottrina dell'apartheid, marzo 1961.

August 1966. Charles de Gaulle, president of the French Fifth Republic, mingles with crowds in Addis Abeba, Ethiopia, during his world tour. He had just visited the Liberation Memorial, where he received a better reception than he would have been given in Algeria.

Agosto de 1966. Charles de Gaulle, presidente de la Quinta República francesa, se mezcla con las masas en Addis Abeba, Etiopía, durante su viaje alrededor del mundo. Acababa de visitar el monumento conmemorativo de la liberación, donde fue mejor recibido que en Argelia.

Agosto 1966. Charles de Gaulle, presidente della Quinta Repubblica francese, fa un bagno di folla ad Addis Abeba, in Etiopia, durante il suo viaggio intorno al mondo. Aveva appena visitato il monumento della Liberazione, dove aveva trovato un'accoglienza migliore di quella che gli sarebbe stata riservata in Algeria.

Harold Wilson, British prime minister, 1968. Wilson, too, had his African problems. In November 1965, Ian Smith unilaterally declared Rhodesia (now Zimbabwe) an independent state.

Harold Wilson, primer ministro británico, en 1968. Wilson también tuvo sus problemas con África. En noviembre de 1965, Ian Smith declaró unilateralmente la independencia de Rhodesia (hoy Zimbabwe).

Harold Wilson, primo ministro inglese, 1968. Anche Wilson aveva i suoi problemi africani. Nel novembre del 1965, Ian Smith dichiarò unilateralmente l'indipendenza della Rodesia (oggi Zimbabwe).

2. Conflict
Conflictos bélicos
Conflitti

One of the many haunting images from the bloodiest war of the decade. A US infantryman carries a wounded refugee from the carnage of Vietnam, 25 October 1968. It was the year in which millions of Americans, appalled by what they had seen on television, began to doubt that the United States would win.

Una de tantas imágenes espantosas de la guerra más sangrienta de la década. Un soldado de la infantería norteamericana lleva en brazos a una refugiada herida para alejarla de la carnicería de Vietnam, el 25 de octubre de 1968. Aquél fue el año en que millones de estadounidenses, horrorizados por las imágenes transmitidas por la televisión, empezaron a dudar de la victoria de EE.UU.

Una delle molte raccapriccianti immagini della più sanguinosa guerra della decade. Un soldato americano trasporta una rifugiata vietnamita, 25 ottobre 1968. Fu in quell'anno che milioni di americani, indignati dalle immagini diffuse dalle televisioni, iniziarono a dubitare nella vittoria degli Stati Uniti.

2. Conflict
Conflictos bélicos
Conflitti

The world had at last recovered from World War II. Europe and Japan had been rebuilt. The cars, luxury goods, food and money that had been in short supply in the immediate post-war years of the Forties and Fifties were now flooding the markets. It was time for new conflicts.

The Sixties were the years when everyone took sides – when, for a while, everyone lived in everyone else's backyard. It didn't matter where the riots, wars and revolutions were raging. It didn't matter who you were – Khrushchev, Kennedy or a complete unknown. What mattered was how each struggle was resolved. Many believed they were living through the opening salvoes of the final showdown between Capitalism and Communism, freedom and totalitarianism.

Much of Europe teetered on the brink of revolution. Most of southern Africa was on the brink of a bloodbath. Within a few years, the stability of France was threatened first by the extreme Right, and then by the extreme Left. The struggle for independence tore Algeria, Kenya, Cyprus, Aden and Nigeria apart.

By the time the dust settled in Sharpeville, My Lai, Prague, the Golan Heights, Nicosia, Leopoldville and the Bay of Pigs, a new and frightened world had been created.

El mundo se había recuperado, por fin, de la II Guerra Mundial. Europa y Japón habían sido reconstruidos. Coches, productos de lujo, alimentos y dinero, bienes que habían escaseado durante las décadas inmediatas de posguerra —los años cuarenta y cincuenta—, invadían ahora los mercados. Eran tiempos para nuevos conflictos.

En los años sesenta todo el mundo tomaba partido por algo y, durante algún tiempo, todo el mundo espiaba a su vecino. No importaba dónde se desencadenaran los disturbios, las guerras y las revoluciones. Tampoco importaba quién era cada cual: Jruschov, Kennedy o un completo desconocido. Lo fundamental era el modo de resolver cada conflicto. Muchos creían estar viviendo los inicios del enfrentamiento decisivo entre capitalismo y comunismo, libertad y totalitarismo.

Gran parte de Europa estaba al borde de una revolución. Casi toda Sudáfrica se hallaba cerca de un baño de sangre. En pocos años, la estabilidad de Francia se vio amenazada, primero por la extrema derecha, y luego por la extrema izquierda. La lucha por la independencia destrozó a Argelia, Kenia, Chipre, Adén y Nigeria.

Cuando por fin se respiró la tranquilidad en Sharpeville, My Lai, Praga, en los Altos del Golán, Nicosia, Leopoldville y la bahía de Cochinos, había nacido ya otro mundo nuevo y asustado.

Il mondo era uscito da poco dal secondo conflitto mondiale. La ricostruzione dell'Europa e del Giappone era appena stata portata a termine. Le automobili, i prodotti di lusso, il cibo e il denaro di cui c'era stata tanta scarsità negli anni Quaranta e Cinquanta stavano ora invadendo i mercati. Era suonata l'ora di nuovi conflitti.

I Sessanta furono gli anni in cui non ci si poteva non schierare da una parte o dall'altra. Poco importava dove esplodevano le rivolte, le guerre e le rivoluzioni. Poco importava se si era Krusciov, Kennedy o un perfetto sconosciuto. Ciò che contava era il modo in cui ogni conflitto si risolveva. Molti erano convinti di assistere agli ultimi soprassalti del capitalismo, allo scontro finale tra la libertà e il totalitarismo.

Gran parte dell'Europa era sull'orlo della rivoluzione. In quasi tutti i paesi dell'Africa meridionale stavano per esplodere sanguinosi conflitti. Nel volgere di pochi anni la stabilità della Francia si ritrovò a essere minacciata prima dall'estrema destra e poi dall'estrema sinsitra. La lotta per l'indipendenza insanguinò Algeria, Kenya, Cipro, Aden nello Yemen e la Nigeria.

Quando a Sharpeville, a My Lai, a Praga, sulle colline del Golan, a Nicosia e nella Baia dei Porci ritornò la calma, era nato un nuovo e spaventoso mondo.

Palestine refugees cross the Allenby Bridge over the River Jordan during the Six-Day War, June 1967. The bridge had been blown up to hinder pursuit by Israeli troops but, in a series of lightning attacks, the Israelis gained control of the West Bank.

Refugiados palestinos cruzan el puente Allenby sobre el río Jordán durante la guerra de los Seis Días, junio de 1967. El puente había sido volado para frenar el avance de las tropas israelíes pero, tras una serie de ataques relámpago, éstas se hicieron con el control de la orilla oeste.

Rifugiati palestinesi attraversano il ponte Allenby, sopra il fiume Giordano, durante la guerra dei Sei giorni, giugno 1967. Il ponte era stato fatto saltare per ostacolare l'inseguimento delle truppe israeliane, che con una serie di azioni lampo erano però riuscite a conquistare la sponda occidentale.

An Israeli soldier studies a burning oil refinery on the Egyptian side of the Suez Canal, June 1967. 'We are making mincemeat of everything on the ground,' reported Mordechai Hod, an Israeli Air Force commander.

Un soldado israelí observa el incendio de una refinería de petróleo en el lado egipcio del canal de Suez, junio de 1967. "Hacemos picadillo todo cuanto encontramos", declaró Mordechai Hod, comandante de las fuerzas aéreas israelíes.

Un soldato israeliano guarda una raffineria in fiamme sul lato egiziano del canale di Suez, giugno 1967. "Sparavamo a tutto ciò che si muoveva", ha dichiarato Mordechai Hod, comandante dell'aviazione israeliana.

Israeli forces with a convoy of Egyptian prisoners during the Six-Day War. The Egyptian army and air force were both humiliated during the war, and Nasser sought to resign as president of the United Arab Republic.

Soldados israelíes con un convoy de rehenes egipcios durante la guerra de los Seis Días. La humillación sufrida por el ejército egipcio y sus fuerzas aéreas hizo que Nasser pensara en dimitir como presidente de la República Árabe Unida.

Soldati israeliani con un convoglio di prigionieri egiziani durante la guerra dei Sei giorni. L'esercito e l'aviazione egiziani furono umiliati e Nasser fu costretto a dimettersi da presidente della Repubblica Araba Unita.

The same city, the same park, the same grass and trees – but two different benches. Salisbury, Rhodesia, during the days of 'separate development', 1967.

La misma gente, el mismo parque, el mismo césped y los mismos árboles, pero dos bancos distintos. Salisbury, Rhodesia, durante la época del plan de "desarrollo separado", en 1967.

Stessa città, stesso parco, stessa erba e stessi alberi, ma due panchine diverse. Salisbury, Rhodesia, all'epoca dello "sviluppo separato", 1967.

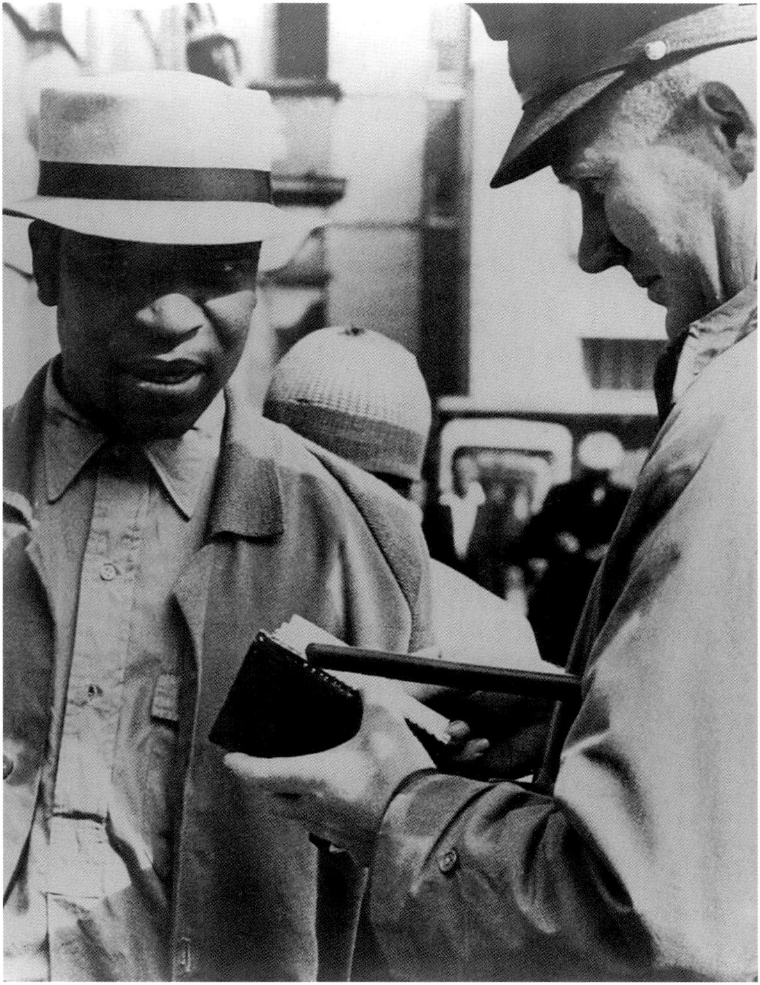

The infamous Pass Laws in operation in South Africa, April 1960. All black citizens had to produce identity passes on demand.

Aplicación de las infamantes *Pass Laws* (leyes de control de identidad) en Sudáfrica, abril de 1960. Cualquier ciudadano negro estaba obligado a mostrar su documento de identidad siempre que le fuera solicitado.

Applicazione delle infami leggi sul controllo dell'identità in Sudafrica, aprile 1960. Tutta la popolazione di colore doveva esibire un tesserino di identità in caso di controllo.

21 March 1960. In Sharpeville, South African police open fire on unarmed protestors, killing 67 and wounding 186.

21 de marzo de 1960. La policía sudafricana abre fuego contra manifestantes desarmados en Sharpeville. Mueren 67 personas y 186 resultan heridas.

21 marzo 1960. A Sharpeville, in Sudafrica, la polizia aprì il fuoco contro manifestanti disarmati uccidendone 67 e ferendone 186.

The *Rhodesia Herald* proudly proclaims Rhodesia's unilateral Declaration of Independence, November 1965. The Prime Minister Ian Smith promised that there would be permanent white minority rule. It lasted just 11 years.

El *Rhodesia Herald* proclama con orgullo la Declaración de Independencia unilateral de Rhodesia, en noviembre de 1965. El primer ministro, Ian Smith, promete que habrá siempre una minoría blanca dirigente. Tan solo duró 11 años.

Il *Rhodesia Herald* orgogliosamente anuncia la Dichiarazione unilaterale d'indipendenza della Rhodesia, novembre 1965. Il primo ministro Ian Smith promise che la minoranza bianca avrebbe continuato a guidare il paese. Il suo governo durò undici anni.

November 1965. Ian Smith walks by Victoria Falls on his first public appearance after the Declaration of Independence. 'I don't believe in black majority rule in Rhodesia…,' he said, '…not in a thousand years.'

Noviembre de 1965. Ian Smith pasea ante las cataratas Victoria en su primera aparición pública tras la Declaración de independencia. "No creo en una mayoría negra dirigente en Rodhesia —dijo— ni siquiera dentro de mil años."

Novembre 1965. Ian Smith, con sullo sfondo le cascate Victoria, nella sua prima apparizione pubblica dopo la Dichiarazione d'indipendenza. "Non credo al governo della maggioranza nera in Rhodesia", disse. "Nemmeno tra mille anni".

April 1967. Still policing the British Empire. A Northumberland Fusilier heavy-handedly imposes law and order in Aden, which had been the first imperial acquisition in Queen Victoria's reign.

Abril de 1967. Aún dura la vigilancia del Imperio británico. Un fusilero de Northumberland impone brutalmente la ley en Adén, la primera colonia imperial de la era victoriana.

Aprile 1967. L'impero britannico mantiene l'ordine. Un fuciliere del Northumberland impone brutalmente la legge ad Aden, prima acquisizione coloniale durante il regno della regina Vittoria.

An Aden civilian crouches in terror as British soldiers threaten him during nationalist demonstrations. The British withdrawal, when it finally came, was a masterly piece of organization.

Un ciudadano de Adén se agacha aterrorizado ante la amenaza de los soldados británicos durante una manifestación nacionalista. La retirada británica, cuando finalmente se produjo, fue una obra magistral de organización.

Un abitante di Aden minacciato da due soldati britannici durante una manifestazione nazionalista. La ritirata britannica, quando finalmente avvenne, fu orchestrata in maniera magistrale.

A French soldier patrols the Casbah, Algiers, during the war of Algerian Independence, 1962.

Soldado francés patrullando por la casba de Argel durante la guerra por la independencia de Argelia, 1962.

Un soldato francese pattuglia la casbah di Algeri durante la guerra d'indipendenza d'Algeria, 1962.

The same Casbah in the uneasy days that followed de Gaulle's ceasefire agreement with the National Liberation Front (FLN), March 1962.

La misma casba durante los tensos días que siguieron al acuerdo de tregua entre De Gaulle y el Frente de Liberación Nacional (FLN), marzo de 1962.

La casbah nei difficili giorni che seguirono l'accordo di cessate il fuoco siglato da de Gaule e dal Fronte di liberazione nazionale (FLN) nel marzo del 1962.

July 1968. A Federal soldier swings a grenade by its release pin as he guards Ibo women and children prisoners during the Biafran War. The war lasted two and a half years, and a million innocent people died of starvation.

Julio de 1968. Un soldado federal sujeta una granada por la anilla mientras vigila a unas mujeres y niños ibo rehenes durante la guerra de Biafra. Esta contienda duró dos años y medio, y en ella murieron de hambre un millón de personas inocentes.

Luglio 1968. Un soldato francese giocherella con la sicura di una bomba a mano mentre sorveglia un gruppo di donne e bambini ibo catturati durante la guerra del Biafra. La guerra durò due anni e mezzo e un milione di innocenti morirono di fame.

Jomo Kenyatta (left) and the Mau Mau leader Field-Marshal Mwariama, 1961. Kenyatta led the independence movement for Kenya, and became its first prime minister. The picture was taken shortly after his release from nine years' imprisonment.

Jomo Kenyatta (izquierda) y el jefe Mau Mau, mariscal de campo Mwariama, en 1961. Kenyatta encabezó el movimiento para la independencia de Kenia y, posteriormente, se convirtió en su primer ministro. Esta fotografía se tomó poco después de su liberación tras nueve años de cárcel.

Jomo Kenyatta (a sinistra) e il capo Mau Mau, il maresciallo Mwariama, 1961. Kenyatta guidò il movimento per l'indipendenza del Kenya e divenne primo ministro del paese. La fotografia è stata scattata poco dopo la sua uscita dal carcere, dove aveva scontato una pena di nove anni.

Don McCullin's photographs from troubled Cyprus. Greek Cypriots, armed with shotguns and primitive British Sten guns, patrol the streets, Nicosia, 1964. The struggle between the Greeks and Turks for control of the island has yet to be resolved.

Fotografías de Don McCullin en un Chipre atormentado. Los grecochipriotas, armados con escopetas y viejos rifles Sten británicos, patrullan por las calles de Nicosia en 1964. La lucha entre turcos y griegos por el control de la isla continúa aún hoy.

Foto di Don McCullin in una Cipro travagliata. Ciprioti greci, armati di fucili e di rudimentali Sten inglesi, patttugliano le strade di Nicosia, 1964. La lotta tra greci e turchi per il controllo dell'isola deve ancora essere risolto.

Limassol, Cyprus, 1964. Mourners cover a casualty in the civil war in Cyprus with the Turkish flag.

Limassol, Chipre, 1964. Los parientes de una víctima de la guerra civil chipriota cubren su cuerpo con la bandera turca.

Limassol, Cipro, 1964. I parenti di una vittima della guerra civile cipriota coprono il corpo con la bandiera turca.

Cypriot widows, victims of the civil war, 1964. A grieving woman (above), whose husband has been killed in the fighting, is comforted by friends. A neighbour (right) brings water to a widow and her child.

Viudas chipriotas, víctimas de la guerra civil, en 1964. Una mujer, cuyo marido ha muerto en el campo de batalla, llora desconsoladamente (superior) y sus amigos tratan de consolarla. Una vecina (derecha) trae agua para una viuda y su hija.

Vedove cipriote, vittime della guerra civile, 1964. Una donna in lacrime (in alto), il cui marito è stato ucciso nel corso dei combattimenti, è confortata dalle amiche. Una vicina (a destra) porta dell'acqua a una vedova e a suo figlio.

Czechoslovakia, August 1968. Hope and terror as the Prague Spring nears its end. The picture was taken shortly after the Soviet invasion with troops from Poland, Hungary, Bulgaria and East Germany.

Checoslovaquia, agosto de 1968. Esperanza y terror cuando la Primavera de Praga toca a su fin. Esta fotografía fue realizada poco tiempo después de la invasión soviética con ayuda de tropas de Polonia, Hungría, Bulgaria y Alemania del Este.

Cecoslovacchia, agosto 1968. Le speranze e i terrori della Primavera di Praga sono finiti. La fotografia è stata scattata subito dopo l'invasione sovietica con soldati polacchi, ungheresi, bulgari e tedeschi dell'Est.

A Soviet tank rolls along the streets of Prague. The Czechs had sought to soften and reform their communist government in a 'socialist democratic revolution'. About 670,000 troops were sent to occupy their country.

Un carro soviético por las calles de Praga. Los checoslovacos intentaron suavizar y reformar su gobierno comunista por medio de una "revolución socialista democrática". Se envió a unos 670.000 soldados para ocupar su país.

Un carro armato russo avanza lungo le strade di Praga. I cechi avevano cercato di costruire un socialismo dal volto umano attraverso una rivoluzione non violenta. Circa 670.000 soldati furono inviati per occupare la Cecoslovacchia.

16 April 1961. Castro's victorious soldiers at (above) the Playa de Citron, and (right) the Playa de Giron, Cuba, after successfully repelling the US backed invasion at the Bay of Pigs. It was a humiliating defeat for the CIA, who had planned and controlled the operation.

El 16 de abril de 1961. Los victoriosos soldados de Fidel Castro (superior) en Playa Larga, y (derecha) Playa Girón, Cuba, tras rechazar el desembarco apoyado por los estadounidenses en la bahía de Cochinos. Supuso una humillante derrota para la CIA, que había planeado y controlado la operación.

16 aprile 1961. I vittoriosi soldati di Fidel Castro sulla Playa de Citron (in alto) e sulla Playa de Giron (a destra), dopo aver respinto l'invasione della Baia dei Porci, sostenuta dagli Stati Uniti. Fu un'umiliante sconfitta per la CIA, che aveva preparato e guidato l'operazione.

II.S

The war in Vietnam escalates, 1965. The flash from a triple salvo of guns on the USS *Canberra* lights up the night sky as they shell the North Vietnamese coast. The previous year the USA had been acting in a purely 'advisory' capacity – with 23,000 troops in South Vietnam.

Escalada de la guerra de Vietnam, 1965. Los destellos de una triple salva de cañones disparada desde el USS *Canberra* iluminan el cielo sobre la costa de Vietnam del Norte. EE.UU. había intervenido el año anterior, únicamente en calidad de "consejero", con 23.000 soldados en Vietnam del Sur.

La guerra del Vietnam esplose nel 1965. Una triplice scarica della cannoniera americana *Canberra* illumina il cielo notturno sulle coste del Vietnam del Nord. L'anno precedente gli Stati Uniti avevano agito in qualità di semplici consiglieri militari, inviando 23.000 soldati nel Vietnam del Sud.

June 1967. An American 175mm projectile blasts from a gun at Camp Carroll in the Qang Tri province, Vietnam.

Junio de 1967. Un proyectil estadounidense de 175 mm es lanzado desde un cañón situado en Camp Carroll, en la provincia de Qang Tri, Vietnam.

Giugno 1967. Un proiettile da 175 mm viene sparato da un cannone americano a Camp Carroll, nella provincia di Qang Tri, in Vietnam.

April 1968. US soldiers take cover in a Vietnam trench near Hill Timothy. This picture is one of a famous set of photographs taken by Terry Fincher.

Abril de 1968. Soldados estadounidenses refugiados tras una trinchera cerca de Hill Timothy. Esta imagen forma parte de una famosa serie de fotografías tomadas por Terry Fincher.

Aprile 1968. Soldati americani si riparano dal fuoco nemico in una trincea nei pressi di Hill Timothy, in Vietnam. Questa fotografia fa parte di una famosa serie scattata da Terry Fincher.

April 1969. Members of the Vietnam National Liberation Front (Vietcong) fire a machine gun at US aircraft during a raid in South Vietnam.

Abril de 1969. Soldados miembros del Frente de Liberación Nacional de Vietnam (Vietcong) disparan con una ametralladora sobre un avión estadounidense durante un bombardeo en Vietnam del Sur.

Aprile 1969. Militanti del Fronte di liberazione nazionale del Vietnam (Vietcong) sparano raffiche di mitragliatrice contro gli elicotteri americani durante un'incursione nel Vietnam del Sud.

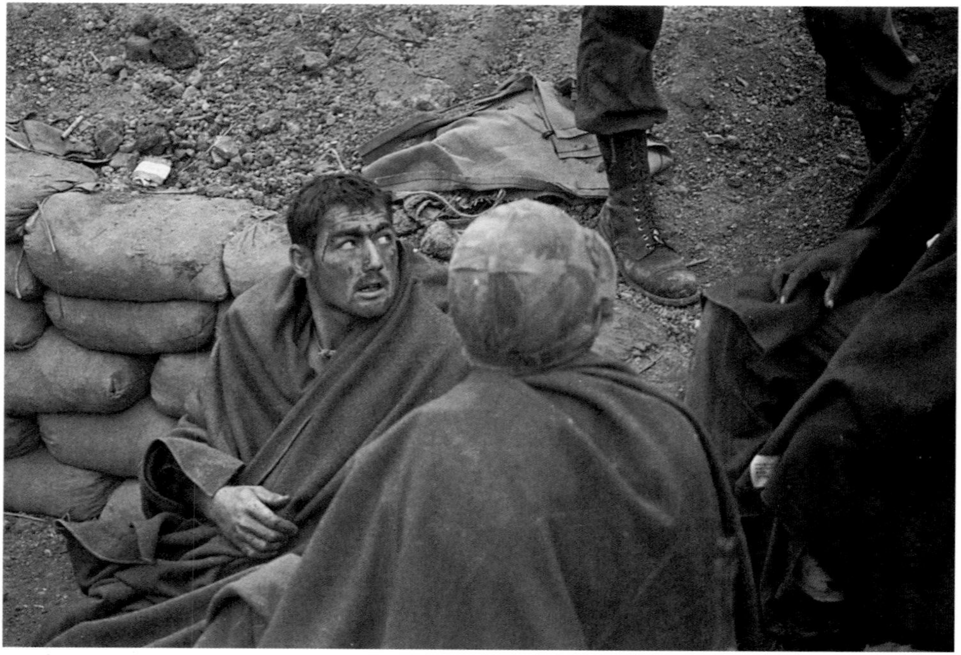

Wounded American soldiers on Hill Timothy, April 1968. Two months earlier, President Johnson had declared at a Washington press conference that the Vietnam Tet offensive was a 'complete failure'.

Soldados estadounidenses heridos en la colina Timothy, abril de 1968. Dos meses antes, el presidente Johnson había declarado en una rueda de prensa en Washington que la ofensiva del Tet había resultado un "completo fracaso".

Soldati americani feriti a Hill Timothy, aprile 1968. Due mesi prima il presidente Johnson aveva dichiarato in una conferenza stampa a Washington che l'offensiva del Tet era stata un "completo fallimento".

October 1968.
Terry Fincher's study of military irony as a skull keeps watch over US soldiers in a Vietnamese jungle camp.

Octubre de 1968.
Terry Fincher documenta la ironía militar. Una calavera monta guardia sobre los soldados estadounidenses en la jungla vietnamita.

Ottobre 1968.
L'ironia militare vista dal fotografo Terry Fincher. Un teschio fa la guardia a un accampamento di soldati americani nella giungla vietnamita.

US troops leap from Sikorsky S-55 helicopters into a swampy field, Vietnam, March 1966. The action was part of a raid to clean out a Vietcong position. The white smoke is from a phosphorous rocket used as a landing marker by a *Bird Dog* observation plane.

Soldados estadounidenses saltan de helicópteros Sikorsky S-55 sobre un campo pantanoso, Vietnam, marzo de 1966. La maniobra formaba parte de un ataque para eliminar una posición Vietcong. El humo blanco procede de un cohete de fósforo lanzado por un avión de reconocimiento *Bird Dog* con el fin de señalar el punto de aterrizaje.

Soldati americani scendono su un terreno paludoso dagli elicotteri Sikorsky S-55, Vietnam, marzo 1966. L'azione faceva parte di un raid per bonificare il territorio dai vietcong. Il fumo bianco proviene da un razzo di segnalazione sparato da un aereo di ricognizione *Bird Dog* per indicare il punto dell'atterraggio.

February 1968. A US Marine weeps in Vietnam, as a helicopter brings back survivors from yet another bloody engagement.

Febrero de 1968. Un soldado de marina estadounidense llora en Vietnam a bordo de un helicóptero de rescate que había recogido a los supervivientes de otro sangriento enfrentamiento.

Febbraio 1968. Un marine in lacrime a bordo dell'elicottero che riporta indietro i sopravvissuti di un'azione costata la vita a molti soldati.

An American soldier drags a frightened man from a hiding place, 1965. The man could have been spy, enemy soldier or innocent civilian. Photographed by Don McCullin.

Un soldado estadounidense arrastra de su escondite a un hombre aterrado, 1965. El individuo podía ser un espía, un soldado enemigo o tal vez un civil inocente. Fotografía de Don McCullin.

Un soldato americano trascina fuori dal suo nascondiglio un vietnamita terrorizzato, 1965. L'uomo poteva essere una spia, un soldato nemico o un innocente civile. Fotografia di Don McCullin.

Crossing a river in the Nghia Hung province, Vietnam, 1967. The US soldier is pushing his combat gear ahead of him on a raft. It was the simplest way to cross the river, but provided little cover from enemy fire.

Cruce a nado de un río en la provincia de Nghia Hung, Vietnam 1967. El soldado estadounidense empuja una armadía que lleva su equipo de combate. Ésta era la forma más simple de cruzar el río, aunque ofrecía escaso cobijo ante el fuego enemigo.

L'attraversamento di un fiume nella provincia di Nghia Hung, Vietnam, 1967. Il soldato americano sta spingendo davanti a sé, su un materassino, la sua tenuta da combattimento. Era il modo più semplice per attraversare il fiume, ma anche il più esposto al fuoco nemico.

Vietnamese refugees crossing the Perfume River, February 1968. The bridge had been destroyed by the military. Terry Fincher's picture is a classic study of one of the saddest scenes from almost any war.

Refugiados vietnamitas cruzan el río Perfume, febrero de 1968. El ejército había destruido el puente. La imagen de Terry Fincher ofrece un estudio clásico de una de las escenas más tristes de todas las guerras.

Rifugiati vietnamiti attraversano il fiume Perfume, febbraio 1968. Il ponte era stato distrutto dai militari. La fotografia di Terry Fincher è paradigmatica nel ritrarre uno dei drammi più comuni a tutte le guerre.

3. Protest Protestas Contestazioni

Martin Luther King, in Birmingham, Alabama, 1963. On 12 April, King and Dr Ralph Abernathy were arrested as they peacefully protested against the racism of Governor George Wallace's regime. Their arrest sparked off violence, and many were injured.

Martin Luther King, en Birmingham, Alabama, 1963. El 12 de abril, King y el Dr. Ralph Abernathy fueron arrestados tras manifestarse pacíficamente en contra del régimen racista del gobernador George Wallace. Su detención originó brotes de violencia, durante los cuales muchas personas resultaron heridas.

Martin Luther King a Birmingham, Alabama, 1963. Il 12 aprile King e il dottor Ralph Abernathy furono arrestati mentre protestavano pacificamente contro il razzismo del governatore George Wallace. Il loro arresto scatenò manifestazioni di violenza, durante le quali vi furono molti feriti.

3. Protest
Protestas
Contestazioni

Whatever poets may say, the child is seldom 'politically' the father of the man. Many of those who spent their Swinging Sixties in flower-bedecked, drug-induced Nirvana later became waspishly intolerant of 'drop-outs'. Similarly, those who raged against authority on the streets of London, Paris, Washington DC, Johannesburg, Limassol, Berlin and a hundred other cities in that revolutionary decade, subsequently suffered changes of political heart and flocked to join their respective 'establishments'.

For a while it seemed the air was full of abuse and tear gas and paving slabs, the streets were alive with the sound of shattering glass, every wall was papered from top to bottom with the posters of exhortation, and every poster was splattered with blood.

But it wasn't all violence. The quiet unflinching dignity of the civil rights marchers in the United States wore down a system that had abused black people for nearly 200 years. In dozens of countries, protesters paraded their opposition to nuclear weapons with a stubbornness that had a half-life at least as long as the radioactivity they abhorred.

Meanwhile, in the wake of the Orange Day parades in July 1969, rioting broke out in many cities in Northern Ireland, and the Sixties began to set the agenda for the Seventies.

Digan lo que digan los poetas, el niño es rara vez el padre "político" del hombre. Muchos de los que vivieron los trepidantes sesenta cubiertos de flores y sumergidos en el nirvana de las drogas se convirtieron más tarde en seres ferozmente intolerantes ante los marginados. Del mismo modo, los que en una década revolucionaria se enfrentaron a las autoridades en las calles de Londres, París, Washington D.C., Johannesburgo, Limassol, Berlín y en cientos de ciudades más, experimentaron después cambios en sus tendencias políticas y recuperaron sus respectivos "puestos en la sociedad".

Durante algún tiempo el aire parecía lleno de abusos, gases lacrimógenos y adoquines; las calles vibraban al son de cristales rotos; no había muro sin empapelar de arriba abajo con carteles que exhortaban a la lucha, y cada cartel estaba salpicado de sangre.

Pero no todo era violencia. La impávida dignidad de los que se manifestaban en defensa de los derechos civiles en EE.UU. desgastaba un sistema que había explotado a los negros durante casi 200 años. En decenas de países, los manifestantes salían a la calle para protestar contra las armas nucleares con una determinación al parecer tan indestructible como la radiactividad que aborrecían.

Mientras tanto, tras las movilizaciones del *Orange Day* en julio de 1969, estallaron disturbios en numerosas ciudades de Irlanda del Norte, que dieron paso a lo que sería la tónica de los años setenta.

Cecché ne dicano i poeti, il bambino è raramente il padre "politico" dell'uomo. La gran parte di coloro che nei favolosi anni Sessanta si vestivano di fiori ed esploravano i mondi paralleli delle droghe, è diventata a sua volte intollerante nei confronti delle minoranze. Quanto a coloro che in quei turbolenti anni erano scesi nelle strade di Londra, Parigi, Washington D.C., Johannesburg, Limassol, Berlino e altre città per protestare contro il potere costituito, non tardarono a cambiare di spalla il loro fucile per ricongiungersi alla buona borghesia dalla quale provenivano.

Per un po', l'aria fu satura di gas lacrimogeni, le strade risuonarono del rumore delle vetrine infrante dai sanpietrini e tutti i muri furono ricoperti di graffiti che incitavano alla rivolta.

Ma la violenza non era tutto. Negli Stati Uniti, la stoica dignità dei manifestanti del movimento per i diritti civili consentì loro di mettere sotto accusa un sistema che aveva sfruttato i neri per quasi due secoli. In decine di paesi i pacifisti manifestarono contro le armi nucleari, con una determinazione indistruttibile come la radioattività contro la quale protestavano.

Infine, dopo i cortei degli orangisti nel luglio 1966, esplosero rivolte in molte città dell'Irlanda del Nord, preannunciando quello che sarebbe stato il clima degli anni Settanta.

The French tricolour flies high over crowds marching to the Arc de Triomphe during the heady days of May 1968. At times up to 10,000 students fought the CRS riot police on the streets of Paris.

La bandera tricolor francesa ondea sobre las multitudes que desfilan en una manifestación hacia el Arco del Triunfo durante los agitados días de mayo de 1968. En alguna ocasión hasta 10.000 estudiantes se enfrentaron a la CRS (policía antidisturbios) en las calles de París.

Il tricolore francese sventola sopra i manifestanti che sfilano verso l'Arco di Trionfo nei giorni caldi del maggio 1968. Fino a 10.000 studenti si scontrarono con la polizia nelle strade di Parigi.

Daniel Cohn-Bendit, leader of the students' strike and more familiarly known as 'Danny the Red', addresses a street meeting at the Gare de l'Est, Paris, 14 May 1968.

Daniel Cohn-Bendit, líder de la huelga de estudiantes y más conocido como "Danny el Rojo", pronuncia un discurso durante una asamblea en la estación del Este, París, 14 de mayo de 1968.

Daniel Cohn-Bendit, leader degli scioperi studenteschi e più noto con il nome di "Danny il rosso" interviene in un'assemblea di strada alla Gare de l'Est, Parigi, 14 maggio 1968.

'...But put your faith in tear gas...' Though faced by overwhelming opposition, a member of the Paris CRS hurls a gas canister to disperse a section of the crowd that had gathered on May Day, 1968.

"... Pon tu fe en los gases lacrimógenos..." A pesar de estar solo ante la abrumadora multitud, un miembro de la CRS de París lanza una granada de gases lacrimógenos para dispersar a parte de un grupo de manifestantes, 1 de mayo de 1968.

"...E abbiate fiducia nei gas lacrimogeni..." Da solo di fronte a un'immensa folla ostile, un poliziotto francese lancia un candelotto lacrimogeno per disperdere i manifestanti il 1° maggio 1968.

The fighting in Paris lasted for nearly four weeks. Buses and cars were overturned and set ablaze. 422 people were arrested. Over 600 were seriously injured. Here, a casualty is led away from one of the many battles.

Los disturbios en París duraron cerca de cuatro semanas. Se volcaron e incendiaron coches y autobuses, y 422 personas fueron arrestadas. Unas 600 resultaron gravemente heridas. En la foto, una herida es retirada de una de las numerosas contiendas.

Gli scontri a Parigi durarono quasi quattro settimane. Autobus e automobili furono rovesciati e incendiati. 422 persone furono arrestate e oltre 600 furono gravemenrte ferite. Qui sopra, una dimostrante ferita viene fatta allontanare dal teatro degli scontri.

Paris, 7 May 1968. Some of the worst fighting took place in the Latin Quarter. Students hurl paving stones at police in the Rue St Jacques. The police respond with yet more tear gas.

París, 7 de mayo de 1968. Los peores enfrentamientos ocurrieron en el Quartier Latin. Los estudiantes lanzan ladrillos contra la policía en la calle Saint Jacques. La policía responde con gases lacrimógenos.

Parigi, 7 maggio 1968. Gli scontri più duri ebbero luogo nel quartiere latino. Gli studenti lanciano porfido contro la polizia in rue St. Jacques, la polizia risponde con i lacrimogeni.

April 1968. American National Guardsmen patrol the smouldering streets of Washington DC in the riots that followed the murder of Martin Luther King.

Abril de 1968. La guardia nacional estadounidense patrulla por las devastadas calles de Washington D.C. tras los altercados que siguieron al asesinato de Martin Luther King.

Aprile 1968. La guardia nazionale americana pattuglia le strade di Washington D.C., devastate dalle rivolte esplose dopo l'assassinio di Martin Luther King.

Police arrest an injured rioter during civil rights disturbances in Newark, New Jersey, August 1964.

La policía detiene a un manifestante herido durante las protestas a causa de la lucha por los derechos civiles en Newark, Nueva Jersey, agosto de 1964.

La polizia arresta un dimostrante ferito durante gli incidenti provocati dal movimento per i diritti civili a Newark, New Jersey, agosto 1964.

Time out from rioting, USA, 1961. Although most blacks supported Martin Luther King's non-violent methods, there were those who agreed with Robert F Williams, who urged: 'We must fight back.'

Un descanso en los enfrentamientos, EE.UU., 1961. Aunque muchos negros apoyaban los métodos no violentos de Martin Luther King, también había quienes estaban de acuerdo con Robert F. Williams, quien clamaba: "Debemos contraatacar".

Lontano dai disordini, USA, 1961. Nonostante molti neri sostenessero i metodi non violenti di Martin Luther King, non mancavano i seguaci di Robert F. Williams, il cui slogan era: "Dobbiamo rispondere colpo su colpo."

Beaufort, South Carolina, May 1965. Members of the Ku Klux Klan take the oath of loyalty to white supremacy.

Beaufort, Carolina del Sur, mayo de 1965. Miembros del Ku Klux Klan juran lealtad a la supremacía blanca.

Beaufort, Carolina del Sud, maggio 1965. Neoadepti del Ku Klux Klan prestano il giuramento di fedeltà alla supremazia bianca.

Four women cheer the first Martin Luther King-led civil rights march from Selma, Alabama to the State Capital, Montgomery, March 1965. One of the leaders of the movement, Bernard Lafayette, described the bravery of some of Selma's citizens: 'No matter how bad a place is, some people got courage.'

Cuatro mujeres aplauden la primera marcha en defensa de los derechos civiles dirigida por Martin Luther King desde Selma, Alabama, hasta Montgomery, capital del estado, en marzo de 1965. Uno de los líderes del movimiento, Bernard Lafayette, describió así la valentía de algunos de los ciudadanos de Selma: "A pesar de lo terrible que llegue a ser un lugar, siempre habrá gente con coraje".

Quattro donne salutano il passaggio di Martin Luther King alla prima marcia per i diritti civili, da Selma, Alabama, alla capitale dello stato, Montgomery, marzo 1965. Uno dei leader del movimento, Bernard Lafayette elogiò il coraggio dei cittadini di Selma: "Anche là dove la situazione è terribile, ci sono delle persone coraggiose".

Four men idly watch the same march pass by. There was little they had to do to beat back the marchers – that was done for them by Sheriff Jim Clark and his deputies, and the Alabama state troopers.

Cuatro hombres contemplan ociosos el paso de la misma marcha. No podían hacer demasiado para dispersar a los manifestantes: el sheriff Jim Clark y sus ayudantes, así como los soldados del estado de Alabama, ya se encargaban de ello.

Quattro uomini assistono pigramente al passaggio della stessa marcia. C'era poco da fare contro la dimostrazione: ci penseranno lo sceriffo Jim Clark, i suoi assistenti e i soldati dello stato dell'Alabama, a respingere i manifestanti.

Black Panther national chairman Bobby Seale (left), with 'defence minister' Huey Newton. They were the founders of the Black Panther movement in 1966.

El presidente nacional de los Panteras Negras, Bobby Seale (izquierda), junto al "ministro de defensa" Huey Newton. Ambos fundaron el movimiento de los Panteras Negras en 1966.

Il capo delle Pantere Nere Bobby Seale (a sinistra), con il suo "ministro della difesa" Huey Newton. Entrambi furono tra i fondatori del movimento delle Pantere Nere nel 1966.

The black activist Malcolm X, 1965. In the previous year he had left the Black Muslims to set up the Organization of Afro-American Unity (OAAU). He called for a revolution, and taught that 'there can be no revolution without bloodshed'. He was murdered in February 1965.

El activista negro Malcolm X, 1965. Un año antes había abandonado a los Musulmanes Negros para fundar la Organización para la unidad afroamericana (OAAU). Malcolm X buscaba una revolución y declaraba que "no puede existir revolución sin derramamiento de sangre". Fue asesinado en febrero de 1965.

L'attivista nero Malcolm X, 1965. L'anno precedente aveva abbandonato i Musulmani neri per fondare l'Organizzazione dell'unità afroamericana (OAAU). Era convinto che fosse giunto il momento di una rivoluzione e sosteneva che "non vi può essere rivoluzione senza spargimento di sangue". Malcolm X fu assassinato nel febbraio del 1965.

Over 200,000 people (left) gather near the Washington Memorial in August 1963 to demand equal rights for 20 million black Americans, and to hear a speech by Dr Martin Luther King. King is seen (above) in discussion with President Johnson, a year later.

Más de 200.000 personas (izquierda) se reúnen en agosto de 1963 alrededor del monumento conmemorativo a Washington para reclamar la igualdad de derechos para los 20 millones de negros americanos y escuchar el discurso del Dr. Martin Luther King. Un año más tarde, King (superior) se entrevistó con el presidente Johnson.

Oltre 200.000 persone (a sinistra) si dettero convegno nei pressi del Washington Memorial nell'agosto del 1963 per chiedere la parità di diritti per 20 milioni di neri americani e ascoltare un discorso di Martin Luther King. Qui sopra, Martin Luther King discute con il presidente Johnson un anno più tardi.

A woman holds up a swastika during a fascist demonstration in Trafalgar Square, London, June 1962.

Una mujer alza una esvástica durante una manifestación fascista en Trafalgar Square, Londres, junio de 1962.

Una donna esibisce il disegno di una svastica durante una manifestazione fascista a Trafalgar Square, Londra, giugno 1962.

Big on banners, small on supporters. British Nazis wave the flag at another rally in Trafalgar Square, one month later.

Muchas banderas pero pocos seguidores. Los nazis británicos ondean su bandera en otra concentración en Trafalgar Square, un mes más tarde.

Sotto imponenti cartelli, gli scarsi aderenti al partito nazista inglese agitano le loro bandiere a un altro raduno a Trafalgar Square, un mese più tardi.

March 1962.
London police carry off an anti-nuclear demonstrator who had staged a sit-down protest in Parliament Square.

Marzo de 1962. La policía londinense se lleva a la fuerza a una manifestante que participaba en una sentada contra el uso de las armas nucleares en Parliament Square.

Marzo 1962.
La polizia inglese allontana una dimostrante antinucleare durante un sit-in di protesta a Parliament Square.

March 1963. CND supporters on one of their many 'Ban the Bomb' marches from London to Aldermaston.

Marzo de 1963. Simpatizantes del movimiento antinuclear CND en una de sus numerosas marchas de "fuera bombas" desde Londres a Aldermaston.

Marzo 1963. Aderenti al movimento antinucleare durante una marcia "contro la Bomba" da Londra a Aldermaston.

An anti-Vietnam war protester kicks a policeman during the Grosvenor Square riot outside the American Embassy in London, 3 July 1966. Violence flared on both sides.

Un manifestante en contra de la guerra de Vietnam propina una patada a un policía durante los disturbios en Grosvenor Square a las puertas de la embajada estadounidense en Londres, 3 de julio de 1966. La violencia se dio por ambos lados.

Un dimostrante contro la guerra del Vietnam prende a calci un poliziotto inglese durante gli scontri del 3 luglio 1966 a Grosvenor Square, davanti all'ambasciata americana a Londra. La violenza esplose da entrambi i lati.

Police cordons attempt to hold back crowds at the same riot. Although many of the demonstrators were said to be students, protest against the war came from many groups and generations.

Cordones policiales intentan contener a las multitudes en la misma sublevación. Aunque se decía que la mayoría de los manifestantes eran estudiantes, distintos grupos y generaciones se unieron en la protesta contra la guerra.

Cordoni di polizia cercano di trattenere i manifestanti in Grosvenor Square. Anche se la maggior parte dei dimostranti erano studenti, non mancavano i rappresentanti di altri gruppi sociali e di altre generazioni;

Buenos Aires, July 1964. Argentinian police fire tear gas bombs at supporters of Juan Perón. Perón himself had fled to Spain, but the military in Argentina were always fearful that he might be returned to power in an election. In 1966 they assumed power to prevent this.

Buenos Aires, julio de 1964. La policía argentina lanza gases lacrimógenos a los partidarios de Juan Perón. El mismo Perón había huido a España, pero los militares argentinos siempre temieron que volviera al poder tras unas elecciones. Para evitarlo, en 1966 el ejército asumió el poder tras un golpe de Estado.

Buenos Aires, luglio 1964. La polizia argentina lancia gas lacrimogeni contro i sostenitori di Juan Peron. Peron era fuggito in Spagna, ma i militari temevano che potesse tornare al potere, democraticamente eletto. Fu per impedire questo che nel 1966 assunsero il comando.

Italian demonstrators attack a member of the Milan police, April 1969. The incident took place during a rally called by Italian communists.

Manifestantes italianos atacan a un miembro de la policía de Milán, abril de 1969. El incidente ocurrió durante una manifestación organizada por los comunistas italianos.

Militanti dell'estrema sinistra extraparlamentare aggrediscono un poliziotto a Milano, aprile 1969. L'incidente avvenne durante una manifestazione organizzata dai comunisti italiani.

Bernadette Devlin, Independent Unity MP for Mid-Ulster, calls for support during the Battle of the Bogside in Derry (Londonderry), 14 August 1969. Devlin was then the youngest MP in Britain.

Bernadette Devlin, diputada de la Unidad independiente en Mid-Ulster, reclama el apoyo durante la batalla de Bogside en Derry (Londonderry), 14 de agosto de 1969. Devlin era entonces la diputada más joven del Reino Unido.

Bernadette Devlin, deputata irlandese di Unità indipendente parla al megafono durante la battaglia di Bogside a Derry (Londonderry), 14 agosto 1969. La Devlin era all'epoca il più giovane deputato della Gran Bretagna.

The man who needed no megaphone – Ian Paisley, militant Protestant clergyman and founder of the Democratic Unionist Party, in full cry, 22 February 1969. He had just been released from gaol.

El hombre que no necesitaba megáfono: Ian Paisley, activista protestante, pastor y fundador del Partido Unionista Democrático, en pleno discurso, 22 de febrero de 1969. Acababa de salir de la cárcel.

L'uomo che non aveva bisogno di megafono: Ian Paisley, militante protestante, pastore e fondatore del partito Unionista democratico, urla durante una conferenza, 22 febbraio 1969. Paisley era appena uscito di prigione.

Derry youths prepare petrol bombs during the Battle of the Bogside, 12 August 1969. The fighting and burning in this predominantly Catholic area of the city prompted the Ulster Government to call in British troops 'to prevent a breakdown of law and order'.

Jóvenes de Derry preparan cócteles molotov durante la batalla de Bogside, 12 de agosto de 1969. Los enfrentamientos e incendios en este barrio predominantemente católico obligaron al gobierno del Ulster a solicitar la ayuda de las tropas británicas "para prevenir el derrumbamiento de la ley y el orden".

Giovani di Derry preparano bottiglie incendiarie durante la battaglia di Bogside, 12 agosto 1969. Gli scontri e gli incendi in questo quartiere a predominanza cattolica indussero il governo dell'Ulster a chiamare le truppe inglesi per "ripristinare la legge e l'ordine".

One of the rioters hurls a blazing petrol bomb at the height of the battle, August 1969. This conflict marked the beginning of three decades of violence.

Uno de los amotinados lanza un cóctel molotov en el momento álgido de la lucha, agosto de 1969. Este conflicto marcó el principio de tres décadas de violencia.

Un dimostrante lancia una bottiglia incendiaria mentre infuria la battaglia di Bogside, agosto 1969. Questo conflitto segnò l'inizio di tre decenni di violenze.

A member of the Royal Ulster Constabulary fights back, August 1969. A year later the same battle was being fought in the Falls Road, Belfast. Three years later, on Bloody Sunday, it was once again the turn of the Bogside.

Un miembro de la Policía de Irlanda del Norte devuelve el ataque, agosto de 1969. Un año más tarde, la misma batalla se desarrolla en Falls Road, Belfast. Tres años después, se desplaza de nuevo a Bogside, durante el Bloody Sunday (domingo sangriento).

Un agente di polizia dell'Irlanda del Nord si difende dai dimostranti, agosto 1969. Un anno dopo gli scontri infuriarono a Falls Road, a Belfast. E tre anni dopo fu la volta della famosa "Bloody Sunday" (Domenica di sangue).

12 August 1969.
In the Derry struggle, most of the protagonists and most of the victims were young.

12 de agosto de 1969. Los jóvenes constituyeron la mayoría de los protagonistas y de las víctimas de la batalla de Derry.

12 agosto 1969. Nella battaglia di Derry, molti dei protagonisti e molte delle vittime erano adolescenti.

M. QUIGLEY

A dress rehearsal for Bloody Sunday. Violence breaks out between civil rights marchers and members of the Royal Ulster Constabulary, Derry, August 1969.

Ensayo general previo al Bloody Sunday. La violencia estalla entre manifestantes civiles y miembros de la Royal Ulster Constabulary, Derry, agosto de 1969.

Una prova generale prima della Domenica di sangue. Scontri tra i manifestanti per i diritti civili e la polizia dell'Irlanda del Nord, Derry, agosto 1969.

4. Entertainment
Ocio
Spettacolo

Camille Javal, better known as Brigitte Bardot, dances in a scene from one of her later and less successful films, *Two Weeks in September*, October 1966. Bardot's best films were made in the Sixties.

Camille Javal, más conocida como Brigitte Bardot, baila en una escena de una de sus últimas y peores películas, *Dos semanas de septiembre,* octubre de 1966. Bardot interpretó sus mejores películas en los años sesenta.

Camille Javal, meglio nota con il nome di Brigitte Bardot, in una scena di uno dei suoi ultimi film, *Deux semaines en septembre*, ottobre 1966. La Bardot aveva interpretato i suoi film migliori negli anni Sessanta.

4. Entertainment
Ocio
Spettacolo

The cinema industry found itself in crisis in the Sixties. Television had destroyed its old confidence and had stolen its traditional audience. Television was cheap, accessible, and quick to produce – a new pop star could be on screen before the ink had dried on his contract. Film-making was comparatively slow and cumbersome, and very expensive.

So Hollywood bounced back by spending ever more money. *Ben Hur* won 11 Oscars in 1960 and set the pattern for much of the decade. Epics that followed included *El Cid*, *Lawrence of Arabia* and *Cleopatra*. More humbly, the British film industry kept going with a series of anti-hero films *(Saturday Night and Sunday Morning*, *This Sporting Life*, *Alfie)*, but was shaken if not stirred when Bond came along.

Darryl F Zanuck gambled on recouping the losses he had suffered over *Cleopatra* with profits he hoped to make with *The Sound of Music*. He won. Hitchcock lost his touch but made his money with *Psycho*, *The Birds* and *Marnie*. Visconti accused 20th Century-Fox of 'destroying' *The Leopard* when they cut it from four hours to two and a half.

Towards the end of the decade, Hollywood abandoned history and entered new alien worlds with *2001: A Space Odyssey* and *Planet of the Apes*.

La industria del cine sufrió una crisis en los sesenta. La televisión había destruido su vieja seguridad y le había arrebatado su público habitual. La pequeña pantalla era barata, accesible y de producción inmediata: una nueva estrella de la música pop podía aparecer en escena antes de que se secara la tinta de su contrato. La realización cinematográfica era en comparación lenta, complicada y muy costosa.

Ante tal situación, Hollywood se recuperó invirtiendo más dinero que nunca. *Ben Hur* consiguió 11 *oscars* en 1960 e instauró el modelo a seguir por la gran mayoría de películas de la década. Otras películas épicas posteriores fueron *El Cid*, *Lawrence de Arabia* y *Cleopatra*. Algo más modestamente, la industria cinematográfica británica continuó produciendo películas de antihéroes *(Sábado noche y domingo mañana, El ingenuo salvaje, Alfie)*, pero recibió una sacudida, o más bien sufrió una conmoción, con la llegada de James Bond.

Darryl F. Zanuck apostó por las ganancias que esperaba obtener con *Sonrisas y lágrimas* para recuperar las pérdidas de *Cleopatra,* y ganó. Hitchcock perdió algo de genialidad pero consiguió dinero con *Psicosis*, *Los pájaros* y *Marnie la ladrona*. Visconti acusó a la 20th Century-Fox de "destruir" *El gatopardo* al recortarla de cuatro a dos horas y media.

Hacia finales de la década, Hollywood abandonó la historia por los nuevos mundos alienígenas con *2001: Una odisea del espacio* y *El planeta de los simios*.

Per l'industria del cinema gli anni Sessanta furono un periodo di crisi. La televisione faceva restare a casa il pubblico tradizionale delle sale cinematografiche. La TV era economica, accessibile a tutti e facile da produrre – una nuova star della musica pop poteva nascere sul piccolo schermo prima che si asciugasse l'inchiostro del suo contratto. Mentre la realizzazione di un film era lenta, difficile e molto costosa.

Hollywood decise di rispondere spendendo più di quanto avesse mai fatto nella produzione di superkolossal. Nel 1960 *Ben Hur* vinse ben 11 Oscar, definendo lo stile di quasi tutti i film del decennio. Altre megaproduzioni degli anni Sessanta furono *El Cid, Lawrence d'Arabia* e *Cleopatra*. La più modesta industria cinematografica britannica continuò a produrre film di antieroi (*Sabato sera domenica mattina*, *Io sono un campione*, *Alfie*), prima del rilancio internazionale con l'arrivo di James Bond.

Darryl F. Zanuck mise in cantiere *Tutti insieme appassionatamente* per recuperare le perdite di *Cleopatra*, e vinse la scommessa. Hitchcock perse il suo tocco, ma guadagnò al botteghino con film come *Psycho*, *Gli uccelli* e *Marnie*. Visconti accusò la 20th Century-Fox di avere distrutto *Il gattopardo*, operando tagli che ne avevano ridotto la durata da quattro ore a due ore e mezza.

Verso la fine del decennio, Hollywood abbandonò la storia per volgersi verso i nuovi mondi della fantascienza con film come *2001, Odissea nello spazio* e *Il pianeta delle scimmie*.

Jeanne Moreau at a press conference where she announced her marriage to the fashion designer Pierre Cardin, 1962.

Jeanne Moreau durante una rueda de prensa en la que anunció su compromiso matrimonial con el diseñador de moda Pierre Cardin, 1962.

Jeanne Moreau a una conferenza stampa nel corso della quale annunciò il suo matrimonio con lo stilista Pierre Cardin, 1962.

Romy Schneider on set at the disused Gare St Lazare, Paris, during the filming of Orson Welles' *The Trial*, based on Kafka's novel, 1962.

Romy Schneider en el plató de la abandonada estación de St-Lazare, en París, durante el rodaje de la película de Orson Welles *El proceso*, basada en la novela de Franz Kafka, 1962.

Romy Schneider sul set della Gare St-Lazare, a Parigi, durante le riprese del *Processo* di Orson Welles, tratto dal romanzo di Franz Kafka, 1962.

Peter Sellers and Sophia Loren in what the critics regarded as a travesty of Shaw's comedy, *The Millionairess*, 1960.

Peter Sellers y Sofia Loren en *La millonaria*, película que los críticos consideraron una parodia de la comedia de Bernard Shaw, 1960.

Peter Sellers e Sophia Loren nel film che i critici considerarono una satira della commedia di Shaw, *La milionaria*, 1960.

Marilyn Monroe in *Let's Make Love*, 1960. 'I seem to be a whole superstructure with no foundation,' said Monroe. 'I'm working on the foundation.'

Marilyn Monroe en *El multimillonario*, 1960. "Me siento como un edificio sin cimientos —dijo la Monroe—. Ahora estoy trabajando duro en los cimientos."

Marilyn Monroe in *Facciamo l'amore*, 1960. "Mi sento come una casa senza fondamenta", dichiarò la Monroe. "Ho iniziato a lavorare dalle fondamenta."

Jean-Paul Belmondo arrives at Nice Airport with Ursula Andress, December 1968. He was there to work on *La Sirène du Mississippi* with Catherine Deneuve. The film was later described as 'interesting and uncomfortable'.

Jean-Paul Belmondo llega al aeropuerto de Niza acompañado por Ursula Andress, diciembre de 1968. El actor viajó hasta allí para trabajar en *La Sirena del Mississipi* junto a Catherine Deneuve. La película fue descrita más tarde como "interesante y molesta".

Jean-Paul Belmondo arriva all'aeroporto di Nizza in compagnia di Ursula Andress, dicembre 1968. All'epoca Belmondo stava interpretando *La mia droga si chiama Julie*, al fianco di Catherine Deneuve. Diretto da François Truffaut, il film fu definito dalla critica "interessante e disturbante".

Jane Fonda helps Alain Delon to blow out the 28 candles on his birthday cake, 11 November 1963. They were filming *Ni saints, ni saufs*.

Jane Fonda ayuda a Alain Delon a soplar las 28 velas de su pastel de cumpleaños, 11 de noviembre de 1963. En ese momento rodaban juntos *Ni saints, ni saufs*.

Jane Fonda aiuta Alain Delon a spegnere le 28 candele della sua torta di compleanno, 11 novembre 1963. Fonda e Delon stavano recitando insieme in *Ni saints, ni saufs*.

(Above) Richard Burton takes Elizabeth Taylor's hand at a screening of *Lawrence of Arabia*, 26 March 1963. (Right) Burton and Taylor on the set of *Cleopatra*. 'Acting is a kind of showing off,' said Burton. 'And the best person to show off to is your wife.'

(Superior) Richard Burton junto a Elizabeth Taylor durante una proyección de *Lawrence de Arabia*, 26 de marzo de 1963. (Derecha) Burton y Taylor en el plató de *Cleopatra*. "Actuar es como seducir —dijo Burton—. Y la mejor persona a la que puedes seducir es tu esposa".

(In alto) Richard Burton tiene la mano di Elizabeth Taylor alla prima di *Lawrence d'Arabia*, 26 marzo 1963. (A destra) Burton e Taylor sul set di *Cleopatra*. "Recitare è un po' come sedurre," diceva Burton, "e la persona ideale da sedurre è tua moglie."

Elizabeth Taylor leaves London for California, 27 March 1961. Less than two weeks earlier she had almost died in a London hotel. 'You feel yourself falling into a horrible black pit. You hear a screaming jet noise. Your skin is falling off… I fought so hard to live.'

Elizabeth Taylor deja Londres por California, 27 de marzo de 1961. Poco menos de dos semanas antes estuvo a punto de perder la vida en un hotel londinense. "Tienes la sensación de estar cayendo en un horrible agujero negro. Luego oyes un agudo y prolongado grito. La piel empieza a desprenderse... Luché con todas mis fuerzas por sobrevivir".

Elizabeth Taylor lascia Londra per la California, 27 marzo 1961. Meno di due settimane prima, aveva rischiato la morte in un albergo di Londra. "Ti senti cadere in un orribile pozzo nero. Senti un lungo grido penetrante. La tua pelle si stacca… Ho dovuto battermi con tutte le mie forze per sopravvivere."

Vera Jane Palmer, better known as Jayne Mansfield, 1965. Although many regarded her as a second-rate Marilyn Monroe, Mansfield was an intelligent actress who suffered from being habitually cast as a dumb blonde.

Vera Jane Palmer, más conocida como Jayne Mansfield, en 1965. Aunque muchos la consideraban una Marilyn Monroe de segunda fila, Mansfield era una actriz inteligente que sufrió con frecuencia el hecho de ser relegada a papeles de rubia tonta.

Vera Jane Palmer, meglio conosciuta come Jane Mansfield, 1965. Nonostante molti la considerassero una Marilyn Monroe di seconda classe, Jane Mansfield era un'attrice intelligente che soffriva per il ruolo di bionda svampita che le era stato incollato addosso.

Catherine Deneuve and her husband, the photographer David Bailey, arrive at the Royal Première of *Born Free*, 12 March 1966.

Catherine Deneuve y su marido, el fotógrafo David Bailey, a su llegada al estreno real de *Nacida libre,* el 12 de marzo de 1966.

Catherine Deneuve e il marito, il fotografo inglese David Bailey, arrivano all'anteprima di *Nata libera*, 12 marzo 1966.

Polish film director Roman Polanski and American actress Sharon Tate after their wedding, 20 January 1968. Fifteen months later she was murdered.

El director polaco Roman Polanski y la actriz estadounidense Sharon Tate tras su boda, el 20 de enero de 1968. Quince meses después, ella moriría asesinada.

Il regista polacco Roman Polanski e l'attrice americana Sharon Tate dopo il loro matrimonio, il 20 gennaio 1968. Quindici mesi dopo Sharon Tate venne assassinata.

Steve McQueen and his wife Neile, during a break in the filming of *Bullitt*, August 1968. 'In my own mind,' said McQueen, 'I'm not sure that acting is something a grown man should be doing.'

Steve McQueen y su mujer Neile durante un descanso en el rodaje de *Bullit*, agosto de 1968. "No estoy seguro —dijo McQueen— de que actuar sea algo apropiado para un adulto."

Steve McQueen e la moglie Neile durante una pausa delle riprese di *Bullit*, agosto 1968. "Per quanto mi concerne," ha dichiarato McQueen, "non sono sicuro che quello dell'attore sia un mestiere adatto a un uomo adulto."

Beau Bridges and Lee Grant, on location in Brooklyn during the making of *The Landlord*, September 1969. The film was not a success. 'Not an avenue of offensiveness to any race is left unexplored,' said one critic.

Beau Bridges y Lee Grant durante el rodaje en Brooklyn de *The Landlord*, septiembre de 1969. La película no tuvo demasiado éxito. "No deja nada ni a nadie por ofender", dijo un crítico.

Beau Bridges e Lee Grant durante le riprese di *Il padrone di casa*, a Brooklyn, nel settembre del 1969. Il film non ebbe molto successo. "Nessuna razza era risparmiata dalla sua ironia", commentò un critico.

Woody Allen and Ursula Andress, stars of *What's New Pussycat?*, at the film's Royal Gala Performance, Leicester Square, London, March 1966.

Woody Allen y Ursula Andress, protagonistas de *¿Qué tal, Pussycat?,* durante la gala del estreno de la película en Leicester Square, Londres, marzo de 1966.

Woody Allen e Ursula Andress, interpreti di *Ciao Pussycat*, all'anteprima del film a Leicester Square, Londra, marzo 1966.

Vidal Sassoon gives Mia Farrow a £500 haircut, 1968. Farrow was about to make *Rosemary's Baby*, the first Hollywood film directed by Roman Polanski. The film, about a woman who believes the Devil has fathered her child, repelled, thrilled and fascinated audiences.

Vidal Sassoon le hace un corte de 500 esterlinas a Mia Farrow, 1968. Farrow estaba a punto de rodar *La semilla del diablo,* el primer filme que Roman Polanski dirigía en Hollywood. La película, en la cual una mujer vive convencida de que el diablo es el padre de su hijo, suscitó repulsión, miedo y fascinación entre el público.

Vidal Sassoon fa un taglio di capelli da 500 sterline a Mia Farrow, 1968. L'attrice avrebbe presto interpretato *Rosemary's Baby*, primo film di Roman Polanski a Hollywood. Il film, la storia di una donna che credeva di essere incinta del diavolo, susciterà sentimenti contrastanti nel pubblico.

Judy Garland leaves Heathrow Airport, London, with her fiancé, Micky Deans, 1968. Deans was the manager of Arthur's, a fashionable disco in Manhattan. Garland had come to London to play the Palladium, but she was too sick to work. A year later, she was dead.

Judy Garland sale del aeropuerto de Heathrow, Londres, con su prometido, Micky Deans, 1968. Deans era el gerente de Arthur's, una discoteca de moda en Manhattan. Garland viajó a Londres para cantar en el Palladium, pero su delicado estado de salud se lo impidió. Falleció al año siguiente.

Judy Garland all'aeroporto di Heathrow a Londra insieme al fidanzato Mickey Deans, 1968. Deans era il gestore di Arthur's, un night alla moda di Manhattan. La Garland era venuta a Londra per cantare al Palladium, ma le sue condizioni di salute avevano suggerito di annullare il concerto. Un anno dopo Judy Garland moriva.

Yugoslav actress Sonia Romanoff attacks paparazzo photographer Rino Barillari with an ice cream, Rome, 1966. He had taken an unflattering picture of her.

La actriz yugoslava Sonia Romanoff ataca al *paparazzi* Rino Barillari con un cucurucho, Roma, 1966. El fotógrafo le había tomado una foto poco favorecedora.

L'attrice iugoslava Sonia Romanoff aggredisce il paparazzo Rino Barillari con un gelato, Roma, 1966. Barillari aveva appena scattato una foto poco rispettosa dell'attrice.

The French director Jean-Luc Godard during the filming of *One Plus One*, 1968. The film featured the Rolling Stones, in a plot made up of the parallel themes of 'construction and destruction'. During filming, the studio burnt down.

El director francés Jean-Luc Godard durante el rodaje de *One Plus One*, 1968. En la película, cuyo argumento se basaba en los temas paralelos de "construcción y destrucción", actuaban los Rolling Stones. El estudio se incendió durante el rodaje.

Il regista francese Jean-Luc Godard durante le riprese di *One plus One*, 1968. Il film era interpretato dai Rolling Stones, con una trama basata sul tema parallelo di "costruzione e distruzione". Durante le riprese, lo studio prese fuoco.

Orson Welles, Paris, 1962. 'All of us will always owe him everything' – Jean-Luc Godard on Welles.

Orson Welles, París, 1962. "Todos estaremos siempre en deuda con él", dijo Jean-Luc Godard acerca de Welles.

Orson Welles, Parigi 1962. "Tutti noi gli dovremo sempre qualcosa" ha dichiarato Jean-Luc Godard a proposito di Welles.

A picture by Erich Auerbach of Count Luchino Visconti, 1966. Visconti's two great films of the Sixties were *The Leopard* and *The Damned*. Critics accused him of making films that increasingly looked like operas without music.

El conde Luchino Visconti fotografiado por Erich Auerbach en 1966. Las dos grandes películas de Visconti en los años sesenta fueron *El gatopardo* y *The Damned*. La crítica le acusó de hacer películas cada vez más parecidas a óperas sin música.

Il conte Luchino Visconti ritratto da Erich Auerbach nel 1966. I due grandi film di Visconti negli anni Sessanta futono *Il gattopardo* e *La caduta degli dei*. I critici lo accusarono di fare film che assomigliavano sempre più a opere senza musica.

Federico Fellini at the launch of his film *La Dolce Vita* in Paris, 16 April 1960. The film received critical approval and papal condemnation.

Federico Fellini durante la presentación de su película *La Dolce Vita* en París, 16 de abril de 1960. El filme obtuvo la aprobación de la crítica y la condena papal.

Federico Fellini all'anteprima della *Dolce vita* a Parigi, 16 aprile 1960. Il film destò il consenso della critica e il biasimo del Vaticano.

Founder members of the Rat Pack, Dean Martin (centre) and Frank Sinatra arrive at London Airport, 4 July 1961.

Los miembros fundadores del Rat Pack, Dean Martin (centro) y Frank Sinatra, a su llegada al aeropuerto de Londres, 4 de julio de 1961.

I membri fondatori del *Rat Pack*: Dean Martin (al centro) e Frank Sinatra arrivano all'aeroporto di Londra, 4 luglio 1961.

Another member of the Pack, Sammy Davis Junior (left), with the American comedian Jack Benny, 6 November 1961. They were rehearsing their contributions to the Royal Variety Show at the Prince of Wales Theatre, London.

Otro miembro del Pack, Sammy Davis junior (izquierda), junto al cómico estadounidense Jack Benny, 6 de noviembre de 1961. Ensayaban sus números para el *Royal Variety Show* en el Prince of Wales Theatre de Londres.

Un altro membro del *Rat Pack*, Sammy Davis Junior (a sinistra) con il comediografo americano Jack Benny, durante le prove del loro contributo al Royal Variety Show al Prince of Wales Theatre di Londra, 6 novembre 1961.

December 1964. British actress Diana Rigg as Emma Peel in the cult television series *The Avengers*.

Diciembre de 1964. La actriz británica Diana Rigg interpretando a Emma Peel en la serie de televisión de culto *Los vengadores*.

Dicembre 1964. L'attrice inglese Diana Rigg nel ruolo di Emma Peel nella serie televisiva *Agente speciale*.

James Fox (left) and Mick Jagger on the set of the film *Performance*, 1969. 'You don't have to be a drug addict, pederast, sado-masochist or nitwit to enjoy it,' wrote John Simon, 'but being one or more of these things would help.'

James Fox (izquierda) y Mick Jagger en el plató de la película *Performance,* 1969. "No hay que ser drogadicto, pederasta, sadomasoquista ni imbécil para disfrutar de esta película —escribió John Simon—, pero ser alguna o varias de esas cosas puede ayudar".

James Fox (a sinistra) e Mick Jagger durante le riprese del film *Performance*, 1969. "Non dovete essere necessariamente drogati, pederasti, sadomasochisti o imbecilli per apprezzarlo," ha scritto John Simon, "ma essere l'una o l'altra di queste cose potrà aiutarvi."

'An honest man's word is as good as his bond.' George Lazenby's wasn't very good – here he is relaxing on the set of *On Her Majesty's Secret Service*, November 1968.

"La palabra de un hombre honrado es su máxima garantía". George Lazenby, un mediocre James Bond, descansa en el plató durante el rodaje de *007 al servicio secreto de su Majestad,* noviembre de 1968.

"Nulla vale la parola di un uomo onesto" dice il proverbio. George Lazenby, mediocre progenitore di James Bond, qui ritratto nel novembre del 1968, durante una pausa delle riprese di *Al servizio di Sua Maestà*, non poteve essere definito un "uomo onesto".

Sean Connery's Bond was the best. This is a scene from *You Only Live Twice*, Pinewood Studios, 1966.

Sean Connery fue el James Bond por excelencia. En la foto, escena de *Sólo se vive dos veces*, Pinewood Studios, 1966.

Il Bond di Sean Connery fu il migliore. Qui Bond è in dolce compagnia in *Agente 007 – Si vive solo due volte*, Pinewood Studios, 1966.

Newlyweds Cilla Black and Bobby Willis, 1969. Black had many recording hits in the Sixties, of which perhaps the best-known was *Alfie*. Willis was her manager. Despite appearances here, the marriage has been an extremely happy one over 30 years.

Los recién casados Cilla Black y Bobby Willis, 1969. Black grabó numerosos éxitos musicales en los años sesenta, de los cuales el más conocido sea tal vez *Alfie*. Willis era su representante. Pese a lo que pueda parecer aquí, disfrutaron de un feliz matrimonio durante más de treinta años.

I neosposi Cilla Black e Bobby Willis, 1969. La Black aveva firmato molte canzoni di successo negli anni Sessanta, la più famosa delle quali fu forse *Alfie*. Willis era il suo manager. Nonostante le apparenze è stato un matrimonio molto felice, durato oltre trent'anni.

The English comedian Benny Hill, January 1960. Hill's television programmes became unaccountably popular in many parts of the world.

El cómico inglés Benny Hill, enero de 1960. Los programas de televisión de Hill se hicieron muy populares en todo el mundo.

Il comico inglese Benny Hill, gennaio 1960. I programmi televisivi di Benny Hill diventarono popolari in molti paesi del mondo.

October 1963. British film star Julie Christie (seated) in her Birmingham bedsit. With her is landlady Mrs Dorothy Cetti.

Octubre de 1963. La estrella de cine británica Julie Christie (sentada) en su apartamento de Birmingham junto a su casera, la señora Dorothy Cetti.

Ottobre 1963. L'attrice cinematografica inglese Julie Christie (seduta) nella sua camera ammobiliata di Birmingham con la padrona di casa Mrs Dorothy Cetti.

Michael Caine (centre) with his mother and brother, at home in Bermondsey, London, 1964. Caine was the first of the English working-class romantic screen heroes. 'He has the gift,' wrote Pauline Kael, 'of conveying what his character is thinking without excess motion.'

Michael Caine (centro) con su madre y su hermano en su casa, en Bermonsdey, Londres, 1964. Caine fue el primero de los héroes románticos ingleses de la gran pantalla procedente de la clase trabajadora. "Tiene el don —escribió Pauline Kael— de expresar lo que piensa su personaje sin exagerar sus gestos."

Michael Caine (al centro) con la madre e il fratello nella casa di famiglia a Bermondsey, Londra, 1964. Caine fu il primo eroe romantico del cinema inglese proveniente dalla classe operaia. "Ha il dono," scrisse Pauline Kael, "di comunicare i pensieri del suo personaggio senza movimenti inutili."

5. The Arts
Las artes
Le arti

Rudolf Nureyev, 1967. Nureyev was granted political asylum in Paris in 1961, where he joined the Grand Ballet du Marquis de Cuevas. He made his Covent Garden debut in 1962 with British ballerina Margot Fonteyn, whose career he rekindled.

Rudolf Nureyev, 1967. Nureyev obtuvo asilo político en París en 1961, donde entró a formar parte del Gran Ballet del Marqués de Cuevas. Debutó en el Covent Garden en 1962 junto con la bailarina británica Margot Fonteyn, cuya carrera reavivó.

Rudolf Nureyev, 1967. Nureyev ottenne nel 1961 asilo politico a Parigi, dove entrò a far parte del Grand Ballet du Marquis de Cuevas. Nel 1962 debuttò al Covent Garden con la ballerina inglese Margot Fonteyn, contribuendo al rilancio della sua carriera.

5. The Arts
Las artes
Le arti

In the Sixties, new life was injected into the arts, and new styles developed. There was an air of joyous experimentation that produced the good, the bad and the ugly. Pop artists and Beat poets revelled in the triumph of presentation over content, but it was all rich food for thought. The rock musical *Hair* presented nudity on stage, some attractive songs, and transcendental images that proved to be profitable at the box office.

The art world began to wake up to the fortunes that could be made from paintings. In Paris, an exhibition of Picasso's work in 1967 drew hundreds of thousands of visitors. The National Gallery of Art in Washington DC paid $5 million for *Ginevra dei Benci* by Leonardo da Vinci – then the highest price ever paid for a single painting.

Joseph Heller published *Catch-22* in 1961, and delighted thousands of readers. Rachel Carson published *Silent Spring* in 1962, disturbed many of her readers, and infuriated the agrochemical industry. She died of cancer two years later.

Grandma Moses, the self-trained painter, died at the age of 101. Edith Piaf, the Parisian songstress, died at the age of 47. Andy Warhol was shot by Valerie Solanis, founder of SCUM (the Society for Cutting Up Men), but survived. Ernest Hemingway shot himself, and didn't.

La década de los sesenta fue un período de renovación de las artes y del nacimiento de nuevos estilos. Una época de alegre experimentación de todo tipo: buena, mala y peor. Los artistas pop y los poetas de la generación beat se deleitaban en el triunfo de la forma sobre el contenido, pero suscitaban también motivos de reflexión. El musical de rock *Hair* llevó el desnudo a escena, con algunas canciones pegadizas e imágenes trascendentales que resultaron muy rentables en taquilla.

El mundo del arte comenzó a tomar conciencia de la fortuna que podía hacerse con la pintura. En París, una exposición de la obra de Picasso atrajo a cientos de miles de visitantes en 1967.

La National Gallery of Art de Washington D.C. pagó cinco millones de dólares por el cuadro *Ginevra dei Benci* de Leonardo da Vinci, el precio más alto jamás pagado hasta entonces por un solo cuadro.

Joseph Heller publicó *Trampa-22* en 1961, que cautivó a miles de lectores. Rachel Carson publicó *Primavera silenciosa* en 1962, incomodó a muchos de sus lectores y enfureció a la industria agroquímica. Dos años más tarde, murió de cáncer.

Grandma Moses, la famosa pintora autodidacta, murió a la edad de 101 años. Edith Piaf, la conocida cantante parisiense, murió a los 47. Andy Warhol sobrevivió al disparo de Valerie Solanis, la fundadora de SCUM (la sociedad para descuartizar a los hombres). Ernest Hemingway se disparó a sí mismo, pero no sobrevivió.

Negli anni Sessanta le arti conobbero un nuovo slancio e si svilupparono nuovi stili. Fu un'epoca di gioiose sperimentazioni, che produsse cose buone, meno buone e pessime. Gli artisti pop e i poeti beat fecero trionfare la forma sul contenuto, fornendo nuovo nutrimento alla mente del pubblico. Il musical rock *Hair*, con gli attori nudi in scena, qualche bella canzone e immagini trascendentali, fu un campione di incassi al box office.

Il mondo dell'arte capì all'improvviso che con la pittura ci si poteva arricchire. Nel 1967 una mostra di Picasso a Parigi attirò centinaia di migliaia di visitatori. A Washington D.C. la National Gallery of Art mise in vendita la *Ginevra dei Benci* di Leonardo da Vinci per cinque milioni di dollari – fino ad allora il prezzo più alto mai pagato per un quadro.

Nel 1961 Joseph Heller pubblicò *Comma 22*, che vendette milioni di copie in tutto il mondo. Nel 1962 il libro di Rachel Carson, *Silent Spring*, indignò un gran numero di lettori e provocò una violenta reazione da parte dell'industria agrochimica. L'autrice morì di cancro due anni dopo.

Grandma Moses, la famosa pittrice autodidatta, morì all'età di 101 anni ed Edith Piaf, la celebre cantante parigina, all'età di 47 anni. Andy Warhol sopravvisse alle pugnalate di Valerie Solinas, la fondatrice dello SCUM (Società per la castrazione dei maschi). Ernest Hemingway si sparò e non sopravvisse.

January 1968. American Pop artist Roy Lichtenstein stands in front of his painting *Whaam!*, on show at the Tate Gallery, London. Lichtenstein was a major figure in the Pop art movement, specializing in enlarged versions of pictures from magazines and comic strips.

Enero de 1968. El artista pop estadounidense Roy Lichtenstein posa ante su cuadro *Whaam!*, expuesto en la Tate Gallery, Londres. Lichtenstein fue una de las grandes figuras del pop art y se especializó en enormes ampliaciones de imágenes publicadas en revistas y en tiras de tebeos.

Gennaio 1968. L'artista pop americano Roy Lichtenstein di fronte al suo dipinto *Whaam!*, esposto alla Tate Galery di Londra. Lichtenstein fu uno dei protagonisti della pop art, e si era specializzato negli ingrandimenti di immagini tratte da riviste e da fumetti.

WHAAM!

David Hockney in 1965. Hockney spent much of the Sixties in the United States. He based his series of etchings, *The Rake's Progress*, on his adventures in New York, and taught at the University of California from 1965 to 1967.

David Hockney en 1965. Hockney pasó gran parte de los años sesenta en EE.UU. Su serie de aguafuertes *The Rake's Progress* está basada en sus aventuras neoyorquinas. De 1965 a 1967 fue profesor en la universidad de California.

David Hockney nel 1965. Hockney trascorse la maggior parte degli anni Sessanta negli Stati Uniti, dove insegnò alla University of California dal 1965 al 1967. La serie di incisioni *The Rake's Progress* è direttamente ispirata alle sue avventure a New York.

Pop artist and film-maker Andy Warhol. The Sixties produced some of his most famous work, including the *Campbell's Soup Can* series, and the film *Chelsea Girls*.

El artista pop y realizador cinematográfico Andy Warhol. Durante los años sesenta, Warhol creó algunas de sus obras más famosas, entre las que se incluye la serie *Botes de sopa Campbell* y la película *Chelsea Girls*.

L'artista pop e regista Andy Warhol. Negli anni Sessanta Warhol ha realizzato alcune delle sue opere più famose, compresa la serie dei *Barattoli di minestra Campbell* e il film *Chelsea Girls*.

American author Ken Elton Kesey, May 1969. Kesey was a writer associated with the Beat generation, and author of *One Flew Over the Cuckoo's Nest* (1963), based on his experiences as a ward attendant in a mental hospital.

El autor estadounidense Ken Elton Kesey en mayo de 1969. El escritor Kesey formó parte de la generación beat y escribió *Alguien voló sobre el nido del cuco* (1963), obra basada en sus experiencias como guardia de seguridad en un centro psiquiátrico.

Lo scrittore americano Ken Elton Kesey, maggio 1969. Kesey, rappresentante della Beat generation, è l'autore di *Qualcuno volò sul nido del cuculo* (1963), basato sulla sua esperienza di infermiere in un ospedale psichiatrico.

The high priests of hippiedom. Dr Timothy Leary (centre) in conference with Abbie Hoffman (left) and Jerry Rubin (right), New York City, February 1968.

Los sacerdotes supremos de la doctrina hippy. El Dr. Timothy Leary (centro) durante una conferencia con Abbie Hoffman (izquierda) y Jerry Rubin (derecha), Nueva York, febrero de 1968.

I grandi sacerdoti della cultura hippie. Il dottor Timothy Leary (al centro) durante una conferenza con Abbie Hoffman (a sinistra) e Jerry Rubin (a destra), New York, febbraio 1968.

Norman Mailer (left), American journalist, novelist and polemicist, with writer Henry Miller, 1962. Mailer wrote a series of books against the Vietnam War during the Sixties, including *Why Are We in Vietnam?* and *Armies of the Night*.

Norman Mailer (izquierda), periodista, novelista y agitador estadounidense, junto al escritor Henry Miller, en 1962. En los años sesenta Mailer escribió una serie de libros contra la guerra de Vietnam, entre los cuales se incluyen *Por qué estamos en Vietnam?* y *Los ejércitos de la noche*.

Il giornalista, romanziere e polemista americano Norman Mailer (a sinistra) con lo scrittore Henry Miller, 1962. Negli anni Sessanta Mailer scrisse alcuni libri contro la guerra nel Vietnam, tra i quali *Perché siamo nel Vietnam?* e *Le armate della notte*.

Allen Ginsberg (right) and Gary Snyder, American poets of the Beat generation, 1962. Snyder advocated simple living and hard physical work. Ginsberg advocated experimentation with drugs.

Allen Ginsberg (derecha) y Gary Snyder, poetas estadounidenses de la generación beat, en 1962. Snyder preconizaba la vida sencilla y el trabajo físico duro. Ginsberg abogaba por experimentar con las drogas.

Allen Ginsberg (a destra) e Gary Snyder, poeti americani della beat generation, 1962. Snyder era a favore di una vita semplice e di un duro lavoro fisico, Ginsberg invece sosteneva la sperimentazione delle droghe.

American playwright Arthur Miller, December 1965. In 1961 Miller wrote *The Misfits*, his ex-wife Marilyn Monroe's last film. 'I was prepared to dedicate a year of my life to her enhancement as a performer… I would never have dreamed of writing a movie otherwise.'

El dramaturgo estadounidense Arthur Miller en diciembre de 1965. En 1961 Miller escribió *Vidas rebeldes,* la última película de su ex esposa Marilyn Monroe. "Me proponía dedicar un año entero de mi vida a ensalzarla como actriz... De no ser así, nunca habría soñado con escribir el guión de una película".

Il drammaturgo americano Arthur Miller, dicembre 1965. Nel 1961 Miller scrisse *Gli spostati*, ultimo film della sua ex moglie Marilyn Monroe. "Ero pronto a dedicare un anno della mia vita per valorizzarla come attrice… altrimenti non mi sarei mai messo a scrivere un film".

The Irish playwright Samuel Beckett, Paris, June 1961. Beckett won the Nobel Prize for Literature in 1969.

El dramaturgo irlandés Samuel Beckett, París, junio de 1961. Beckett ganó el premio Nobel de Literatura en 1969.

Il drammaturgo irlandese Samuel Beckett, Parigi, giugno 1961. Nel 1969 Beckett vinse il Nobel per la letteratura.

Beetlemania. Steven Berkoff, British playwright, actor and director, performing in his own adaptation of Kafka's *Metamorphosis* at the Roundhouse Theatre, London, 1969. His role was that of a young man who is transformed into a beetle.

Escarabajomanía. Steven Berkoff, dramaturgo británico, actor y director, interpreta su propia adaptación teatral de *La metamorfosis* de Kafka en el Roundhouse Theatre, Londres, 1969. Representaba el papel de un joven que se transforma en escarabajo.

Insettomania. Il commediografo, attore e regista teatrale Steven Berkoff interpreta il suo adattamento delle *Metamorfosi* di Kafka al Roundhouse Theatre di Londra, 1969. Il suo ruolo era quello di un giovane che si svegliava trasformato in scarafaggio.

Trevor Nunn, successor to Peter Hall as artistic director of the Royal Shakespeare Company, 1968.

Trevor Nunn, sucesor de Peter Hall en la dirección artística de la Royal Shakespeare Company, 1968.

Trevor Nunn, successore di Peter Hall in qualità di direttore artistico della Royal Shakespeare Company, 1968.

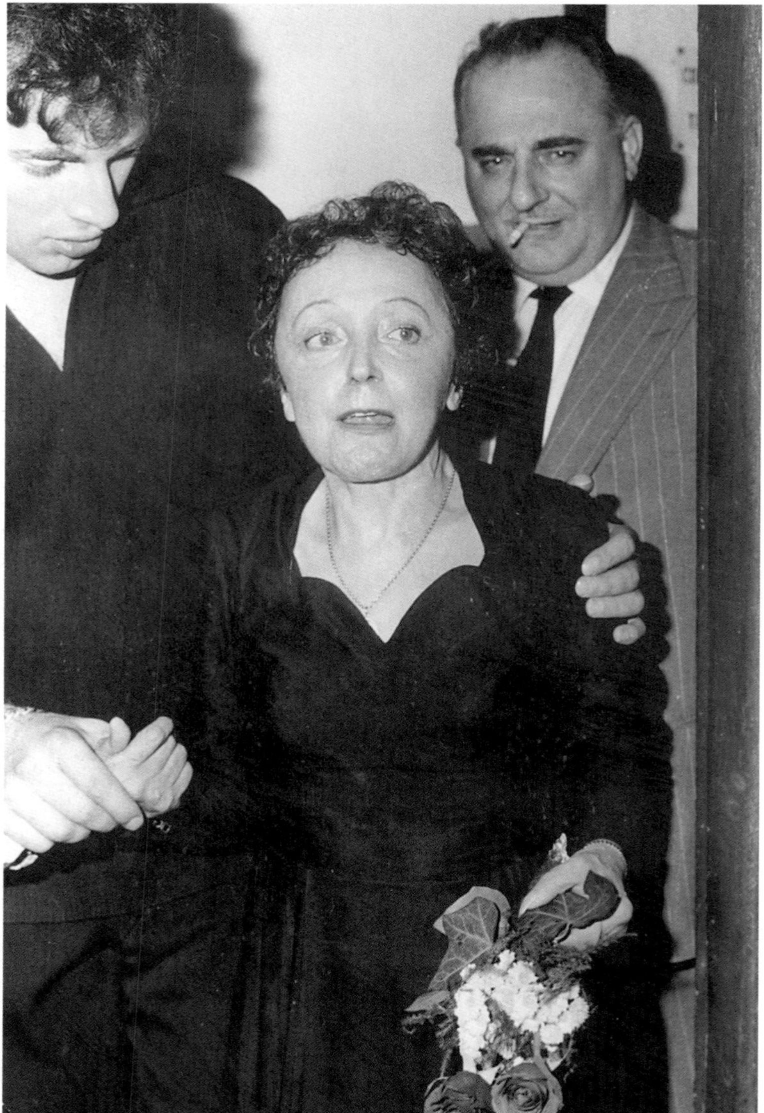

The Little Sparrow – Edith Piaf, perhaps the most popular French singer of all time, 1960.

El pequeño gorrión: Edith Piaf, tal vez la cantante francesa más famosa de todos los tiempos, 1960.

Il passerotto:Edith Piaf, forse la più famosa cantante francese di tutti i tempi, 1960.

The Austrian singer Lotte Lenya, March 1961. Her husky voice was once described as being 'one octave below laryngitis'.

La cantante austríaca Lotte Lenya, marzo de 1961. Su ronca voz fue descrita como "una octava por debajo de la laringitis".

La cantante austriaca Lotte Lenya, marzo 1961. La sua voce roca è stata definita "un'ottava sotto la laringite".

Erich Auerbach's portrait of the jazz pianist, composer and bandleader Thelonious Sphere Monk, April 1961. Monk was a larger-than-life figure, whose humour was revealed in his highly original and percussive style of piano playing.

El pianista, compositor y director de la orquesta de jazz Thelonious Sphere Monk retratado por Erich Auerbach en abril de 1961. Monk era un hombre legendario, cuyo humor se plasmaba en su original forma de tocar el piano.

Il pianista jazz, compositore e direttore di band Thelonius Sphere Monk, fotografato da Erich Auerbach nell'aprile 1961. Monk era un personaggio leggendario, il cui umorismo traspariva dall'originale stile pianistico.

American jazz pianist Dave Brubeck (left) encouraging a young bass player, 1962.

El pianista estadounidense de jazz Dave Brubeck (izquierda) anima a un joven contrabajista, 1962.

Il pianista jazz americano Dave Brubeck (a sinistra) incoraggia un giovane bassista, 1962.

September 1963. A photograph by George Konig of the blind American multi-instrumentalist Roland Kirk. Kirk was in London for a jazz festival.

Septiembre de 1963. George Konig fotografió así al multiinstrumentista estadounidense ciego Roland Kirk, que participó en un festival de jazz celebrado en Londres.

Settembre 1963. Il polistrumentista americano non vedente Roland Kirk fotografato da George Konig durante un festival jazz a Londra.

January 1962. Chet Baker, shortly after his release from prison in Rome. Baker's brillant career as a jazz trumpet player of the cool school was frequently interrupted by drugs charges.

Enero de 1962. Chet Baker, poco después de salir de la cárcel en Roma. Su brillante carrera como trompetista de la escuela de *cool jazz* quedó con frecuencia interrumpida a causa de sus diversas condenas por consumo de drogas.

Gennaio 1962. Chet Baker poco dopo essere stato scarcerato a Roma. La sua brillante carriera di trombettista jazz della scuola *cool* subì varie interruzioni per problemi di droga.

London, 1969. Margot Fonteyn and Rudolf Nureyev during the final rehearsal of a production of the ballet *Pelléas et Mélisande* at the Royal Opera House.

Londres, 1969. Margot Fonteyn y Rudolf Nureyev durante el ensayo general de una producción del ballet *Pelléas et Mélisande*, en la Royal Opera House.

Londra, 1969. Margot Fonteyn e Rudolf Nureyev durante le prove generali del balletto *Pelléas et Mélisande* alla Royal Opera House.

Luciano Pavarotti (left), Joan Sutherland and Spiro Malas in the trio from Donizetti's opera *La Fille du Régiment* at the Royal Opera House, London, 30 May 1966. The photograph is by Erich Auerbach.

Luciano Pavarotti (izquierda), Joan Sutherland y Spiro Malas interpretan el trío de la ópera de Donizetti *La Fille du Régiment* en la Royal Opera House, Londres, 30 de mayo de 1966. Fotografía de Erich Auerbach.

Luciano Pavarotti (a sinistra), Joan Sutherland e Spiro Malas nel trio dell'opera di Donizetti *La figlia del reggimento*, alla Royal Opera House di Londra, 30 maggio 1966. La fotografia è di Erich Auerbach.

Jack Nisberg's striking picture of Maria Callas, Greek-American opera singer, and Aristotle Onassis, Greek millionaire ship owner, 1967.

Una sorprendente fotografía de Jack Nisberg a María Callas, la célebre cantante de ópera greconorteamericana, y al millonario armador griego Aristóteles Onassis, 1967.

La cantante d'opera greco-americana Maria Callas e l'armatore miliardario greco Aristotle Onassis, 1967. Foto di Jack Nisberg.

February 1964.
A portrait by Erich Auerbach of the French composer and conductor Pierre Boulez.

Febrero de 1964.
El compositor y director de orquesta francés Pierre Boulez fotografiado por Erich Auerbach.

Febbraio 1964.
Il compositore e direttore d'orchestra francese Pierre Boulez fotografato da Erich Auerbach.

January 1962.
The English cellist Jacqueline du Pré. She was 17 years old when Auerbach took this picture, but had already made her debut.

Enero de 1962. La violoncelista inglesa Jacqueline du Pré. Tenía sólo 17 años cuando Erich Auerbach la fotografió, pero ya no era una principiante.

Gennaio 1962. La violoncellista inglese Jacqueline du Pré. Aveva solo 17 anni quando venne fotografata da Erich Auerbach, ma non era già più una principiante.

June 1965.
The Russian cellist, conductor and composer Mstislav Leopoldovitch Rostropovich, during a rehearsal.

Junio de 1965.
El violoncelista, director de orquesta y compositor ruso Mstislav Leopoldovich Rostropovich durante un ensayo.

Giugno 1965.
Il violoncellista, direttore d'orchestra e compositore russo Mstislav Leopoldovich Rostropovich durante una prova.

Igor Stravinsky rehearses the BBC Symphony Orchestra, 1961. As a composer, Stravinsky was as prolific as ever in the Sixties.

Igor Stravinski en un ensayo de la Orquesta sinfónica de la BBC, 1961. Stravinski fue un compositor muy prolífico durante los años sesenta.

Igor Stravinskij prova con la BBC Symphony Orchestra, 1961. Negli anni Sessanta Stravinskij fu estremamente prolifico.

London, November 1963. The Russian composer Dmitri Shostakovich during a break in rehearsals of his opera *Katerina Ismailova*.

Londres, noviembre de 1963. El compositor ruso Dmitri Shostakovich durante un descanso en los ensayos de su ópera *Katerina Ismailova*.

Londra, novembre 1963. Il compositore russo Dmitrij Sostakovic durante una pausa nelle prove della sua opera *Katerina Ismailova*.

January 1963. The Russian soprano Galina Vishnevskaya and English composer Benjamin Britten relax during a recording of Britten's *War Requiem*.

Enero de 1963. La soprano rusa Galina Vishnevskaia y el compositor inglés Benjamin Britten en una actitud distendida durante una grabación del *War Requiem* de Britten.

Gennaio 1963. La soprano russa Galina Vishnevskaja e il compositore inglese Benjamin Britten durante una registrazione del *War Requiem* di Britten.

6. Pop
La música pop
La musica pop

Bob Dylan at a press reception in Britain, 3 May 1966. It was the year of Dylan's mysterious disappearance. For over three months, it was said, only the Beat poet Allen Ginsberg knew his whereabouts.

Bob Dylan en una rueda de prensa en el Reino Unido, 3 de mayo de 1966. Aquél fue el año de la misteriosa desaparición de Dylan. Durante más de tres meses se rumoreó que sólo el poeta beat Allen Ginsberg conocía su paradero.

Bob Dylan durante una conferenza stampa in Inghilterra, 3 maggio 1966. Fu questo l'anno della misteriosa scomparsa di Dylan. Per oltre tre mesi, sembra che soltanto il poeta beat Allen Ginsberg conoscesse il suo nascondiglio.

6. Pop
La música pop
La musica pop

There were many who thought (and still think) that Pop was the Sixties. The roll-call of hits and stars reads like a *Who's Who* of popular music – Elvis, Ike and Tina Turner, Sonny and Cher, Little Richard, Little Eva, Buddy Holly, Hendrix, Bo Diddley, Chuck Berry, Jerry Lee Lewis, The Everly Brothers, The Doors, The Crystals, The Ronettes, The Supremes, The Animals, The Bee Gees, The Who… the list goes on for ever.

Behind all the ballyhoo, there were the starmakers – Colonel Parker, George Martin, Larry Page, Phil Spector – those who manufactured the sound or arranged the money.

Never before had music brought such fame. 'If I get any more popular,' said Eric Clapton, 'I shall have to have plastic surgery and get myself a Dr Kildare face.' Never before had record sales been so gross.

At the centre of it all were The Beatles, the four lads from Merseyside, who became the most famous people in the world. The Stones ran them close, but Mick and company were naughty and mischievous, and never straddled the generations as comfortably as John, Paul, George and Ringo. As the decade neared its end, sales of The Beatles' *Abbey Road* album topped four million in two months.

Muchos pensaban (y aún lo piensan) que el pop fue la música que encarnó mejor los años sesenta. La lista de éxitos y estrellas de la época es una especie de "Quién es quién" de la música popular: Elvis, Ike y Tina Turner, Sonny y Cher, Little Richard, Little Eva, Buddy Holly, Hendrix, Bo Diddley, Chuck Berry, Jerry Lee Lewis, The Everly Brothers, The Doors, The Crystals, The Ronettes, The Supremes, The Animals, The Bee Gees, The Who... Todos ellos constituyen una relación interminable.

Tras ese barullo se hallaban los creadores de estrellas —Colonel Parker, George Martin, Larry Page, Phil Spector—, los que producían el sonido y los que distribuían el dinero.

La música no había aportado nunca tantas celebridades. “Si me hago más famoso —dijo Eric Clapton— tendré que someterme a cirugía estética y hacerme una cara como la del Dr. Kildare.” Nunca antes se habían vendido tantos discos.

En el centro de esta vorágine estaban los Beatles, aquellos cuatro muchachos de Merseyside que se convirtieron en las personas más famosas de todo el mundo. Los Stones les seguían muy de cerca, pero Mick y su banda eran traviesos y maliciosos, y nunca cautivaron a generaciones enteras como John, Paul, George y Ringo.

Hacia el final de la década, las ventas del álbum *Abbey Road* de los Beatles superaron los cuatro millones de discos en sólo dos meses.

Per molti la musica pop era (ed è) indissolubilmente legata agli anni Sessanta. D’altronde, i titoli delle canzoni e i nomi delle star di quegli anni costituiscono una sorta di *Who’s Who* della musica pop a venire – Elvis, Ike e Tina Tuner, Sonny and Cher, Little Richard, Little Eva, Buddy Holly, Jimi Hendrix, Bo Diddley, Chuck Berry, Jerry Lee Lewis, The Everly Brothers, The Doors, The Crystals, The Ronettes, The Supremes, The Animals, The Bee Gees, The Who… e l’elenco potrebbe continuare per pagine.

Dietro le strategie pubblicitarie, c’erano i creatori di star – il colonnello Parker, George Martin, Larry Page, Phil Spector – che fabbricavano suoni e incassavano laute percentuali.

Mai la musica aveva reso così famosi. “Se divento ancora più famoso”, ha dichiarato Eric Clapton, “dovrò subire un intervento plastico per farmi fare una faccia alla dottor Kildare”. Le vendite di dischi batterono tutti i record.

Al centro di questo tumulto c’erano i Beatles, i quattro ragazzi di Liverpool che diventarono le persone più famose del mondo. Gli Stones li incalzavano da vicino, ma Mick e la sua banda erano troppo depravati per sedurre intere generazioni, come seppero invece fare John, Paul, George e Ringo. Alla fine del decennio, l’album *Abbey Road* dei Beatles aveva venduto oltre quattro milioni di copie.

With his national service just finished, Elvis Presley describes how his hair was cut in the US army, 1960. He had doubts about whether he could renew his musical career.

Recién terminado su servicio militar, Elvis Presley describe el corte de pelo que le hicieron en el ejército de EE.UU., 1960. Presley ponía en tela de juicio poder reanudar su carrera musical.

1960, terminato da poco il servizio militare, Elvis Presley descrive come gli avevano tagliato i capelli nell'esercito. Si era persino chiesto se avrebbe mai potuto riprendere la carriera musicale.

Elvis and Priscilla Presley leave the Baptist Hospital, Memphis with their baby daughter Lisa-Marie, 10 February 1968.

Elvis y Priscilla Presley a la salida del Baptist Hospital, en Memphis, con su hija Lisa-Marie, el 10 de febrero de 1968.

Elvis e Priscilla Presley lasciano l'ospedale battista di Memphis con la figlia Lisa-Marie, 10 febbraio 1968.

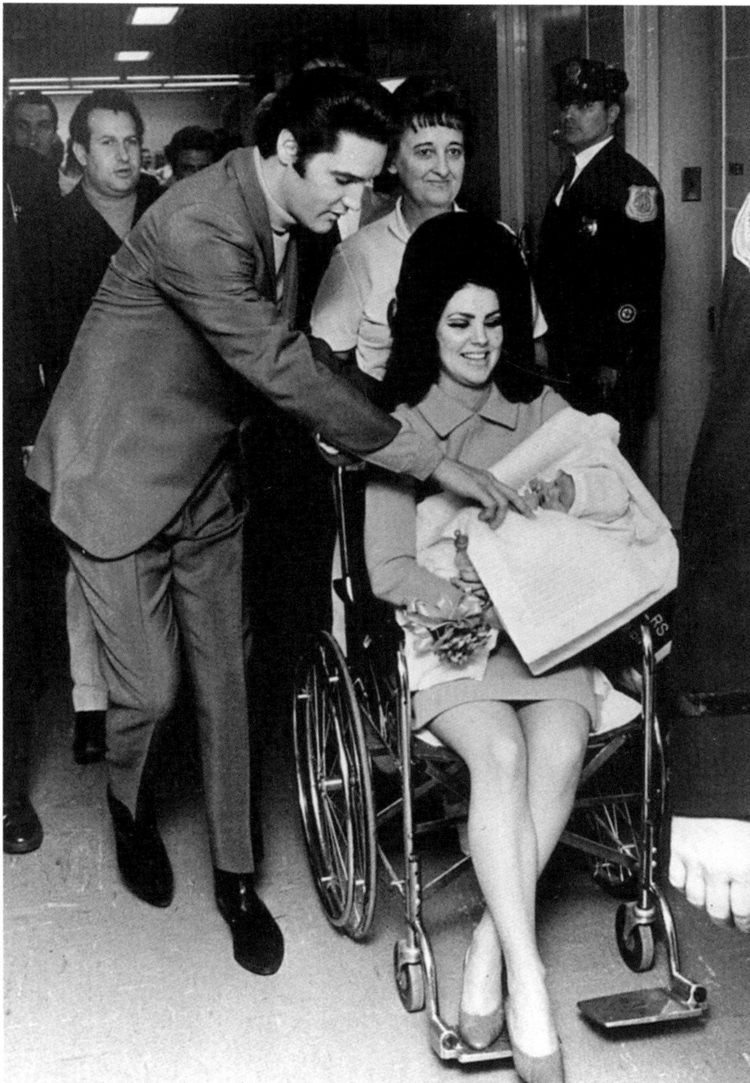

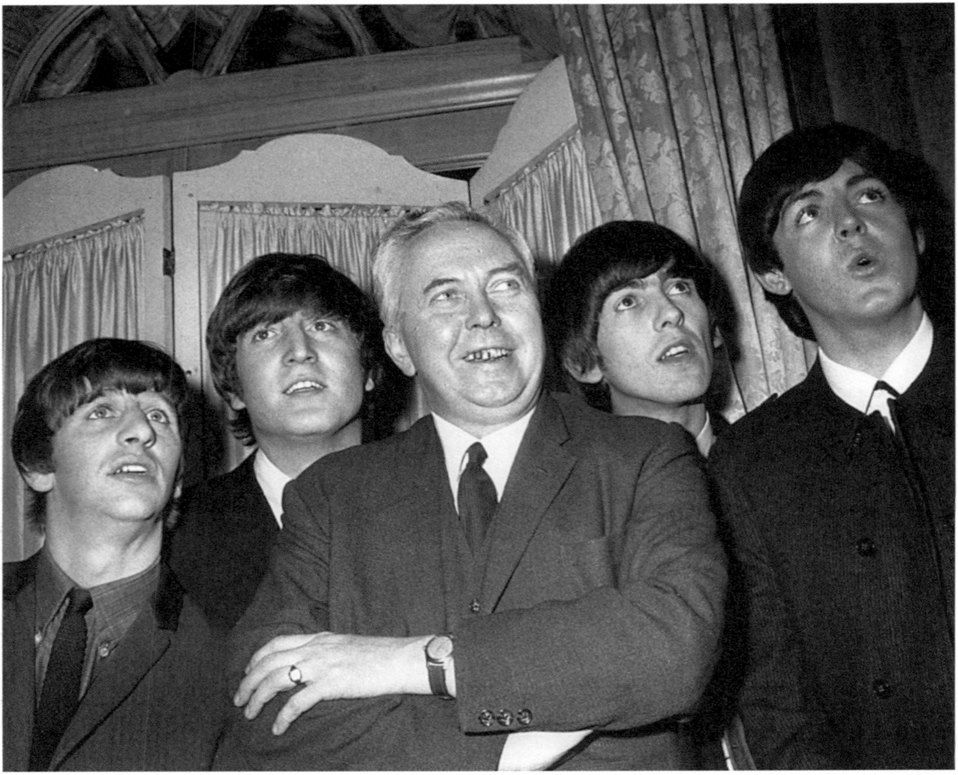

A few months before he became British prime minister, Harold Wilson joins The Beatles at the Dorchester Hotel, London, March 1964. The Fab Four were about to be presented with the Variety Club Award as show business personalities of 1963.

Pocos meses antes de ser nombrado primer ministro, Harold Wilson se reúne con los Beatles en el Dorchester Hotel, Londres, marzo de 1964. Los Fab Four (los cuatro fabulosos) estaban a punto de ser galardonados con el premio Variety Club a las grandes figuras del espectáculo de 1963.

Pochi mesi prima di diventare primo ministro inglese, Harold Wilson si fa fotografare insieme ai Beatles al Dorchester Hotel di Londra, marzo 1964. I Fab Four (i favolosi quattro) stavano per ricevere il Variety Club Award per il loro contributo artistico.

In their early days of fame, the Beatles appear on the stage of the London Palladium, 1963. The audience numbered 2,000 screaming fans – a small gathering compared with what was to come.

Los Beatles en una actuación en el London Palladium, al principio de sus días de gloria, 1963. El público, 2.000 admiradores delirantes, era relativamente escaso comparado con lo que vendría después.

Nei primi anni della loro carriera, i Beatles suonano sul palcoscenico del London Palladium, 1963. Il pubblico contava 2000 fan in delirio, pochi in confronto a quelli degli anni successivi.

Fans attempt to break into the grounds of Buckingham Palace as the Beatles are presented with the Order of the British Empire for their services to music, 26 October 1965.

Una multitud de *fans* intenta romper el cordón policial para entrar en el palacio de Buckingham durante la ceremonia de condecoración de los Beatles con la Orden del Imperio británico por su contribución a la música, 26 de octubre de 1965.

I fan cercano di forzare i cordoni degli agenti a Buckingham Palace durante la cerimonia di conferimento del titolo di baronetti ai Beatles, 26 ottobre 1965.

The Indian influence. Ravi Shankar, Indian composer and sitar player, May 1966. As well as being George Harrison's teacher, Ravi Shankar wrote the film score for Satyajit Ray's *Apu Sansar*.

La influencia india. Ravi Shankar, el compositor y sitarista indio, mayo de 1966. Shankar fue el profesor de George Harrison y compuso la música para la película de Satyajit Ray *Apu Sansar*.

L'influenza indiana. Il compositore e suonatore di sitar indiano Ravi Shankar, maggio 1966. Oltre a essere l'insegnante di George Harrison, Ravi Shankar ha composto la colonna sonora per *La trilogia di Apu* di Satyajit Ray.

The Maharishi Mahesh Yogi instructs John Lennon (left foreground), Maureen Starkey (wife of Ringo Starr) and George Harrison, 1967.

El yogui Maharishi Mahesh instruye a John Lennon (izquierda, primer plano), Maureen Starkey (esposa de Ringo) y George Harrison, 1967.

Il Maharishi Mahesh yogi impartisce i suoi insegnamenti a John Lennon (a sinsitra), Maureen Starkey (moglie di Ringo) e George Harrison, 1967.

Horizontal… John and Yoko in the Amsterdam Hilton, 27 March 1969. They spent a honeymoon week in bed protesting against violence.

En posición horizontal… John y Yoko Ono en el Hilton de Amsterdam, 27 de marzo de 1969. Pasaron su luna de miel de una semana en la cama como protesta contra la violencia.

Orizzontali… John e Yoko all'Amsterdam Hilton, 27 marzo 1969. Avevano trascorso una settimana di luna di miele a letto per protestare contro la violenza.

Vertical… the famous 1968 picture of naked John and Yoko. In the Sixties, people were shocked.

En posición vertical... la famosa fotografía de 1968 con John y Yoko desnudos. Todo un escándalo para la gente de los años sesenta.

Verticali… la famosa fotografia del 1968 di John e Yoko nudi. Negli anni Sessanta questa immagine aveva fatto scalpore.

Paul McCartney and four-year-old Julian Lennon, with John in the background, on holiday near Athens, July 1967.

Paul McCartney y el pequeño Julian Lennon, de cuatro años de edad, con John al fondo, durante unas vacaciones cerca de Atenas, julio de 1967.

Paul McCartney, il piccolo Julian Lennon all'età di quattro anni e John sullo sfondo, in vacanza nei pressi di Atene, luglio 1967.

May 1967. Photographer Linda Eastman (later Linda McCartney) with Paul McCartney at the press launch of *Sergeant Pepper's Lonely Hearts Club Band*. The album was simultaneously released all round the world.

Mayo de 1967. La fotógrafa Linda Eastman (más tarde, Linda McCartney) con Paul McCartney durante la presentación de *Sergeant Pepper's Lonely Hearts Club Band*. El álbum vio la luz simultáneamente en todo el mundo.

Maggio 1967. La fotografa Linda Eastman (poi Linda McCartney) con Paul McCartney alla presentazione alla stampa di *Sergeant Pepper's Lonely Hearts Club Band*. L'album uscì in contemporanea in tutto il mondo.

Mick Jagger (left), with Stones' guitarist Keith Richards, recording music for Jean-Luc Godard's film *One Plus One*, 1968. Their notoriety had increased enormously in 1967 when they were both gaoled for possession of marijuana and four pep pills.

Mick Jagger (izquierda), con el guitarrista de los Stones Keith Richards, grabando la música de la película de Jean-Luc Godard *One Plus One*, 1968. Su fama creció considerablemente cuando fueron encarcelados en 1967 por posesión de marihuana y anfetaminas.

Mick Jagger (a sinistra) con il chitarrista degli Stones Keith Richards durante le riprese del film di Jean-Luc Godard *One Plus One*, 1968. La loro popolarità era enormemente salita nel 1967, quando furono entrambi arrestati per possesso di marijuana e anfetamine.

Paul McCartney during the recording of the soundtrack for *Yellow Submarine*, February 1968. The production assistants appear less impressed than he does.

Paul McCartney durante la grabación de la banda sonora de *Yellow Submarine*, febrero de 1968. Las ayudantes de producción parecen mucho menos impresionadas que él.

Paul McCartney durante la registrazione della colonna sonora di *Yellow Submarine*, febbraio 1968. Le assistenti di produzione non sembrano però molto convinte.

Brian Jones, guitarist with the Rolling Stones, in concert at the Richmond Jazz Festival, 1964. The body of Jones was discovered in his own swimming pool in July 1969.

Brian Jones, guitarrista de los Rolling Stones, durante un concierto en el Richmond Jazz Festival, 1964. Jones fue hallado muerto en su piscina en julio de 1969.

Brian Jones, chitarrista dei Rolling Stones, in concerto al Richmond Jazz Festival, 1964. Il corpo di Jones fu trovato nella sua piscina nel luglio 1969.

A seething and sweating mass of Stones' fans at the Wimbledon Palais, London, August 1964.

Un hervidero de *fans* de los Rolling Stones empapados en sudor en el estadio de Wimbledon, Londres, agosto de 1964.

Fan in delirio si accalcano sotto il palcoscenico durante un concerto degli Stones a Wimbledon, Londra, agosto 1964.

Beauty…
Marianne Faithfull recreates a family portrait with her pet dalmatian, 1964.

La bella... Marianne Faithfull recrea un retrato familiar junto a su perro dálmata, 1964.

La Bella… Marianne Faithfull in posa come in un ritratto di famiglia insieme al suo dalmata, 1964.

...and the Beast. Mick Jagger at the Regent Sound Studio, London, September 1964. The public liked to believe that Faithfull had been corrupted by the Stones.

... y la Bestia. Mick Jagger en el Regent Sound Studio, Londres, septiembre de 1964. Al público le gustaba creer que los Stones habían corrompido a Faithfull.

...e la Bestia. Mick Jagger al Regent Sound Studio, Londra, settembre 1964. Al pubblico piaceva credere che la Faithfull fosse stata corrotta dagli Stones.

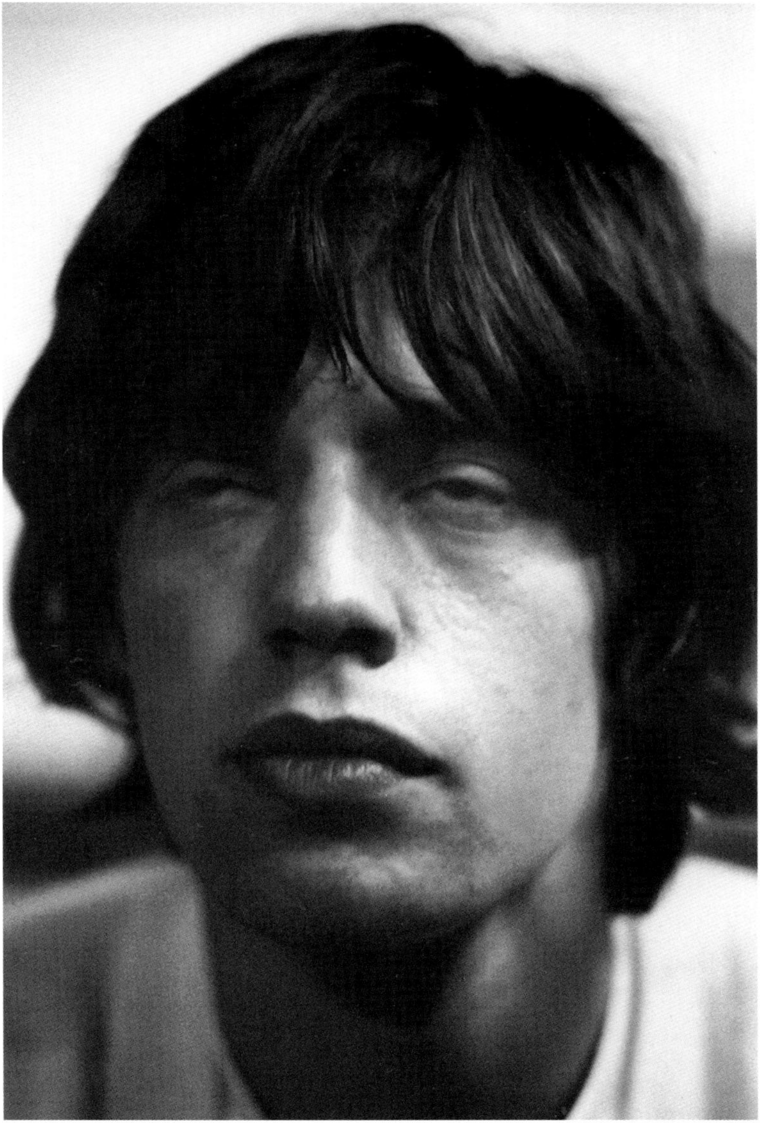

Mick Jagger (left) and Keith Richards leave Wormwood Scrubs Gaol, London, February 1967. They had been released on bail of £7,000, following their drugs charges. The British Establishment was about to shoot itself in the foot.

Mick Jagger (izquierda) y Keith Richards abandonan la prisión de Wormwoods Scrubs, Londres, febrero de 1967. Habían pagado una fianza de 7.000 dólares para librarse de su acusación de posesión de drogas. Las autoridades británicas arrojaban así piedras sobre su propio tejado.

Mick Jagger (a sinistra) e Keith Richards lasciano la prigione di Wormwood Scrubs, Londra, febbraio 1967. Erano stati liberati dietro pagamento di una cauzione di 7000 sterline per possesso di sostanze stupefacenti. Le autorità britanniche avevano commesso un grave errore.

After his trial, Mick Jagger is driven to Brixton Gaol to begin a three-month prison sentence, 30 June 1967. *The Times* newspaper published an editorial the following day, headed: 'Who Breaks a Butterfly on a Wheel?' A week later, Jagger and Richards were released.

Tras ser procesado, Mick Jagger es conducido a la prisión de Brixton para cumplir una pena de tres meses de cárcel, 30 de junio de 1967. El periódico *The Times* publicó un editorial a la mañana siguiente titulado algo así como: "¿No será un juicio demasiado severo para un pequeño delito?". Una semana más tarde, Jagger y Richards fueron liberados.

Dopo il processo, Mick Jagger viene trasferito alla prigione di Brixton per scontare la sentenza di tre mesi di carcere, 30 giugno 1967. Il giorno dopo *The Times* pubblicò un editoriale intitolato: "Un giudizio troppo severo per un piccolo crimine". Una settimana più tardi Jagger e Richards furono rilasciati.

The British singer Dusty Springfield on stage, April 1969. She had many hits in the Sixties, notably 'I Only Want To Be With You' and 'You Don't Have to Say You Love Me'.

La cantante británica Dusty Springfield en el escenario, abril de 1969. Muchas de las canciones de Springfield fueron éxitos de los sesenta, sobre todo "I Only Want To Be With You" y "You Don't Have to Say You Love Me".

La cantante inglese Dusty Springfield sul palcoscenico, aprile 1969. Negli anni Sessanta interpretò numerose canzoni di successo tra le quali si ricordano "I Only Want To Be With You" e "You Don't Have to Say You Love Me".

Taking a break from singing – Sandie Shaw models clothes in the window of her London boutique, September 1967.

En un descanso como cantante, Sandie Shaw hace de maniquí en el escaparate de su tienda en Londres, septiembre de 1967.

Lontano dalle luci della ribalta. La cantante Sandie Shaw gioca a fare la modella nella vetrina della sua boutique a Londra, settembre 1967.

Little Stevie Wonder, with harmonica, March 1965. He was 14 years old, and beginning to taste success.

El pequeño Stevie Wonder con su armónica, marzo de 1965. Tenía catorce años y empezaba a saborear el éxito.

Il giovane Stevie Wonder, con l'armonica, marzo 1965. All'epoca aveva 14 anni e iniziava a conoscere il successo.

18 March 1965. Martha and the Vandellas in concert on the *Sound of Motown* television channel. Douglas Jeffery took this picture and the two following, all on the same day.

18 de marzo de 1965. Martha y las Vandellas durante un concierto en el canal de televisión *Sound of Motown*. Douglas Jeffery tomó esta fotografía y las dos siguientes en el mismo día.

18 marzo 1965. Martha e the Vandellas in concerto sul canale televisivo *Sound of Motown*. Douglas Jeffrey scattò questa fotografia e la successiva nello stesso anno.

Smokey Robinson and the Miracles. The Detroit-based Motown Corporation outsold all other American record companies in 1965, with stars that included Marvin Gaye, the Four Tops and the Temptations.

Smokey Robinson y los Miracles. La casa discográfica de Detroit Motown Corporation dejó atrás a las demás compañías estadounidenses, en 1965, con estrellas como Marvin Gaye, los Four Tops y las Temptations.

Smokey Robinson e The Miracles. Nel 1965 la casa discografica di Detroit Motown Corporation diventò la numero uno in America con star come Marvin Gaye, i Four Tops e The Temptations.

Diana Ross, another *Sound of Motown* star, and lead singer of the Supremes. The group had five straight number one hits in 1964 and 1965.

Diana Ross, otra estrella de la *Sound of Motown* y solista de las Supremes. El grupo obtuvo cinco éxitos número uno entre 1964 y 1965.

Diana Ross, un'altra star della *Sound of Motown* e cantante solista delle Supremes. Il gruppo salì ai vertici delle hit parade nel 1964 e 1965.

American blues rock singer Janis Joplin, live on stage, 1969. She died of a drugs overdose the following year.

La cantante estadounidense de blues Janis Joplin en una actuación en directo, 1969. Murió de sobredosis al año siguiente.

La cantante blues americana Janis Joplin, durante uno spettacolo, 1969. L'anno seguente morì di overdose.

Sonny (Salvatore Bono) and Cher (Cherilyn Sarkasian La Pier) on honeymoon in Britain, August 1965.

Sonny (Salvatore Bono) y Cher (Cherilyn Sarkasian La Pier) en su luna de miel en el Reino Unido, agosto de 1965.

Sonny (Salvatore Bono) e Cher (Cherilyn Sarkasian La Pier) in luna di miele in Inghilterra, agosto 1965.

The American pop singer Marsha Hunt, September 1969. After famously disrobing in the stage musical *Hair* and claiming that Mick Jagger was the father of her daughter Karis, Hunt went on to become a successful novelist.

La cantante pop estadounidense Marsha Hunt, septiembre de 1969. Tras escandalizar al público con su famoso desnudo en el musical *Hair* y declarar que Mick Jagger era el padre de su hija Karis, Hunt se convirtió en una novelista de fama.

La cantante pop americana Marsha Hunt, settembre 1969. Dopo essersi spogliata in scena nel musical *Hair,* affermò che Mick Jagger era il padre di sua figlia Karis. Marsha Hunt divenne in seguito una scrittrice di successo.

Britain's finest white soul singer, Joe Cocker, in mid-song at the Isle of Wight Festival, 11 September 1969.

El mejor cantante de soul blanco del Reino Unido, Joe Cocker, en concierto en el festival de la isla de Wight, 11 de septiembre de 1969.

Il migliore cantante soul inglese bianco, Joe Cocker, in concerto sul palcoscenico del Festival dell'isola di Wight, 11 settembre 1969.

Pop singer David Jones, later and better known as David Bowie, 1965. Bowie's Sixties' *Space Oddity* was notable in that he accompanied himself with a toy Stylaphone on the hit single.

El cantante pop David Jones, más tarde y mejor conocido como David Bowie, 1965. Su álbum de los años sesenta *Space Oddity* destacó en especial porque Bowie se acompañó de un juguete Stylaphone en su sencillo de mayor éxito.

Il cantante pop David Jones, successivamente meglio conosciuto come David Bowie, 1965. In uno dei suoi successi degli anni Sessanta, *Space Oddity*, cantava accompagnandosi con uno strumento giocattolo Stylaphone.

Marc Bolan, lead singer with T Rex, 1965. Bolan was one of the leaders of the Glam Rock school of Pop, which became immensely popular at the beginning of the Seventies.

Marc Bolan, solista de T Rex, 1965. Bolan fue uno de los líderes del movimiento pop *glam rock,* muy popular a principios de la década de los setenta.

Marc Bolan, cantante solista dei T Rex, 1965. Bolan fu uno degli esponenti di spicco del cosiddetto “glam rock” britannico, che diventò molto di moda all’inizio degli anni Settanta.

7. Fashion
Moda
Moda

October 1965. Jean Shrimpton in Medusa mode, displaying a 'sun' hairstyle designed by the Parisian stylist, Carita.

Octubre de 1965. Jean Shrimpton con el estilo medusa luce un corte de pelo "sol" diseñado por el peluquero y estilista parisiense Carita.

Ottobre 1965. Jean Shrimpton stile Medusa mostra un'acconciatura "solare" dello stilista parigino Carita.

7. Fashion
Moda
Moda

It was as though the fashion world had suddenly discovered colour and freedom. A kaleidoscopic liberation took place after centuries of restriction. It was epitomized by the miniskirt – one small piece of material for a woman, one giant leap for womankind.

Men, too, had one of those brief periods in history when they could strut about in rich plumage. The streets of the West were thronged with dedicated followers of fashion, in Italian suits, in floral shirts, in hippie furs and flowing kaftans.

Designers and models became celebrities. People who cared little for fashion knew all about Mary Quant, Jean Shrimpton and Twiggy. Carnaby Street and the King's Road were familiar names to millions who had never been near London. The designs flowed from the drawing boards of top couturiers, and the mass-produced variations on the designs filled the rails of the chain stores and boutiques.

Some predicted that it would lead to a collapse of morals, to anarchy – or worse, to joy. The Pill and the miniskirt seemed to promise some kind of Shavian Utopia, providing the maximum of temptation with the maximum of opportunity.

It never came, but it was fun while it lasted.

El mundo de la moda parecía haber descubierto de repente el color y la libertad de estilo en los años sesenta. Tras varios siglos de restricciones, se produjo una liberación calidoscópica personificada por la minifalda: una pequeña prenda para una mujer, pero un gran paso para el mundo femenino.

También los hombres disfrutaron de uno de esos breves períodos históricos en que podían pavonearse vestidos con ricos plumajes. Las calles de Occidente aparecían atestadas de fervientes seguidores de la moda que lucían trajes italianos, camisas floreadas, abrigos de piel hippies y flotantes caftanes.

Los diseñadores y sus modelos se hicieron famosos. Incluso la gente que no se interesaba demasiado por la moda lo conocía todo sobre Mary Quant, Jean Shrimpton y Twiggy. Los nombres de Carnaby Street y King's Road resultaban familiares para millones de personas que jamás habían visitado Londres. La moda era diseñada por los más célebres modistos, y las imitaciones en masa de sus diseños llenaban los estantes de los grandes almacenes y las tiendas de ropa.

Algunos predijeron que todo ello conduciría al hundimiento de la moral y a la anarquía o, lo que era peor, a la felicidad. La píldora y la minifalda parecían prometer aquella especie de utopía imaginada por Bernard Shaw, que proporcionaba las máximas tentaciones junto con el máximo de oportunidades.

Ninguna predicción se cumplió, pero resultó divertido mientras duró.

Fu come se il mondo della moda avesse improvvisamente scoperto il colore e la libertà, una caleidoscopica liberazione dopo secoli di restrizioni. Il fenomeno fu esemplificato dalla minigonna: un pezzo di tessuto che costituì un enorme passo avanti per le donne.

Anche gli uomini conobbero uno di quei brevi periodi nella storia della moda in cui poterono pavoneggiarsi con la massima disinvoltura. Le strade dell'Occidente erano affollate di fedeli seguaci della moda, con abiti italiani, camicie a fiori, pellicce hippie o ampi caffetani.

Stilisti e modelle diventarono delle celebrità. Anche la gente comune, che non seguiva la moda, sapeva tutto su Mary Quant, Jean Shrimpton e Twiggy. Carnaby Street e King's Road erano nomi familiari a milioni di persone che non erano mai state a Londra. Dopo essere stati disegnati dai grandi sarti, i modelli venivano copiati in mille modi e prodotti industrialmente per finire sui banchi dei grandi magazzini e delle boutique.

Alcuni predicevano che tutto questo avrebbe portato alla fine dell'ordine morale, all'anarchia o, peggio ancora, alla felicità. La pillola e la minigonna sembravano annunciare un'utopia immaginata da Bernard Shaw, con infinite tentazioni e opportunità.

L'utopia non si realizzò mai, ma finché durò fu divertente.

September 1969. Yves St Laurent, flanked by two of his fashion models, Betty Calroux (left) and Lucie de la Falaise. St Laurent opened his own fashion house in 1962, and launched the first of his Rive Gauche boutiques in 1966.

Septiembre de 1969. Yves Saint Laurent entre dos de sus modelos, Betty Calroux (izquierda) y Lucie de la Falaise. Saint Laurent fundó su propia casa de alta costura en 1962, y abrió la primera de sus tiendas Rive Gauche en 1966.

Settembre 1969. Yves Saint Laurent con due delle sue modelle, Betty Calroux (a sinistra) e Lucie de la Falaise. Saint Laurent aprì la sua casa di moda nel 1962 e inaugurò la prima delle sue boutique sulla Rive Gauche nel 1966.

The Sixties stylist. Mary Quant arrives at Buckingham Palace to collect her OBE, 15 November 1966.

La estilista de los años sesenta. Mary Quant acude al palacio de Buckingham para recoger su condecoración de la Orden del Imperio británico (OBE), 15 de noviembre de 1966.

La stilista degli anni Sessanta Mary Quant arriva a Buckingham Palace per ricevere la decorazione dell'Ordine dell'Impero britannico (OBE), 15 novembre 1966.

The smile of the Sixties. Meagher's portrait of one of the most famous fashion models of the age, Jean Shrimpton, July 1966.

La sonrisa de los sesenta. El retrato de Meagher de una de las modelos más famosas de la época, Jean Shrimpton, julio de 1966.

Il sorriso degli anni Sessanta. Una delle più famose modelle del periodo, Jean Shrimpton, luglio 1966. Foto di Meagher.

An icon of the Sixties. Lesley Hornby, better known as Twiggy, 1967. In the background is boyfriend Justin de Villeneuve.

Un icono de los años sesenta. Lesley Hornby, más conocida como Twiggy, 1967. En segundo plano, su novio Justin de Villeneuve.

Un'icona degli anni Sessanta. Lesley Hornby, meglio nota come Twiggy, insieme al fidanzato Justin de Villeneuve, 1967.

May 1966. Twiggy stands on the back of a car to model a transparent plastic halterneck dress.

Mayo de 1966. Twiggy posa en la parte trasera de un coche descapotable con un vestido de plástico transparente de espalda desnuda.

Maggio 1966. Twiggy in posa sul bagagliaio di un'auto con un abito di plastica trasparente.

The scene is Chelsea. The time is August 1967. The mood is one of confidence and happiness. The boots are made for walking…

Esta escena se desarrolla en Chelsea, agosto de 1967, en una atmósfera de confianza y felicidad. Las botas están hechas para caminar...

La scena si svolge a Chelsea, nell'agosto 1967. L'atteggiamento è di fiducia e felicità. Gli stivali sono fatti per camminare…

April 1967. A swaggering Sixties pose and a coat designed by Paco Rabanne. The coat is made of triangular pieces of leather, to look like chain-mail.

Abril de 1967. Pose arrogante de los años sesenta y abrigo de Paco Rabanne. La prenda está hecha con piezas triangulares de cuero que imitan una cota de malla.

Aprile 1967. Un'arrogante posa, molto anni Sessanta, e un giaccone disegnato da Paco Rabanne, realizzato con triangoli di pelle per creare un effetto cotta di maglia.

February 1967.
Twiggy displays one item from a fashion collection that she was about to launch in the United States.

Febrero de 1967.
Twiggy muestra uno de los modelos de la colección que se disponía a presentar en EE.UU.

Febbraio 1967.
Twiggy indossa un capo di una collezione che si apprestava a lanciare negli Stati Uniti.

It was almost the mini-mac, and the hats were known as 'pork-pies'. Two nattily dressed gents step out, May 1967.

Los impermeables casi minis y los sombreros *pork-pies* (pasteles de carne). Dos jóvenes elegantemente vestidos listos para dar una vuelta, mayo de 1967.

Una versione quasi-mini di impermeabile abbinata con cappelli denominati "pork pies" (torte di carne). La tenuta ideale per una piovosa giornata londinese, maggio 1967.

April 1968. Two hippies set out on the road to Swinging London.

Abril de 1968. Dos hippies camino del Swinging London.

Aprile 1968. Due hippie in cammino per la Swinging London.

Two samples from the Spring hat collection of London designer Edward Mann, February 1966. On the left is 'Sea Diver', a vinyl helmet with a perspex earphone. On the right is 'Seaspray', a red and white racing cap with a sun-protecting visor.

Dos sombreros de la colección de primavera del diseñador londinense Edward Mann, febrero de 1966. A la izquierda, "Sea Diver", un gorro de vinilo con orejas de plexiglás. A la derecha, "Seaspray", una gorra de ciclista rojiblanca con visera para protegerse del sol.

Due copricapi della collezione primavera di Edward Mann, stilista londinese, febbraio 1966. A sinistra, "Tuffatore", elmetto di vinile con copriorecchie di perspex. A destra "Mare spray", cappello bianco e rosso con visiera antisole.

A futuristic helmet of 1966, protection against some of the mighty cold winters in the Sixties.

Gorro futurista de 1966, para protegerse de los terriblemente fríos inviernos de los años sesenta.

Un futuristico copricapo del 1966, ideale per proteggersi dai freddi inverni degli anni Sessanta.

It wasn't all miniskirt… it wasn't all clumpy platform heels. Roy Jones took this picture of a model wearing a paper dress, February 1967.

No todo eran minifaldas... ni enormes zapatos de plataforma. Roy Jones fotografió a esta modelo, que lucía un vestido de papel, en febrero de 1967.

Non solo minigonne… e super-zatteroni. Una modella con un abito di carta fotografata da Roy Jones nel febbraio 1967.

The false eyelashes are made from fake flower petals and real hair. The lipstick, the whole makeover, is vintage Sixties.

Pestañas postizas hechas con pétalos de flores artificiales y pelo auténtico. El pintalabios y todo el maquillaje resultan muy típicos de los años sesenta.

Le ciglia false sono state realizzate con petali di plastica e peli autentici. Il rossetto e tutto il trucco sono estremamente tipici degli anni Sessanta.

On the roof of the Carlton House Towers, London, a model wears a trouser suit made entirely of white feather boas, 1967.

En el tejado del Carlton House Towers, Londres, una modelo viste un traje pantalón realizado por completo con plumas blancas de boa, 1967.

Sul tetto del Carlton House Towers, a Londra, una modella indossa un abito realizzato interamente con piume bianche, 1967.

'To boldly go where no fashion designer has gone before...' A swimsuit for the space age, modelled by Judy Fairbairn, September 1969.

"Aventurarse hasta allí donde nunca se atrevió a estar antes ningún diseñador..." Traje de baño para la era espacial presentado por Judy Fairbairn, septiembre de 1969.

"Avventurarsi là dove nessuno stilista ha osato avventurarsi...". Costume da bagno spaziale indossato da Judy Fairbairn, settembre 1969.

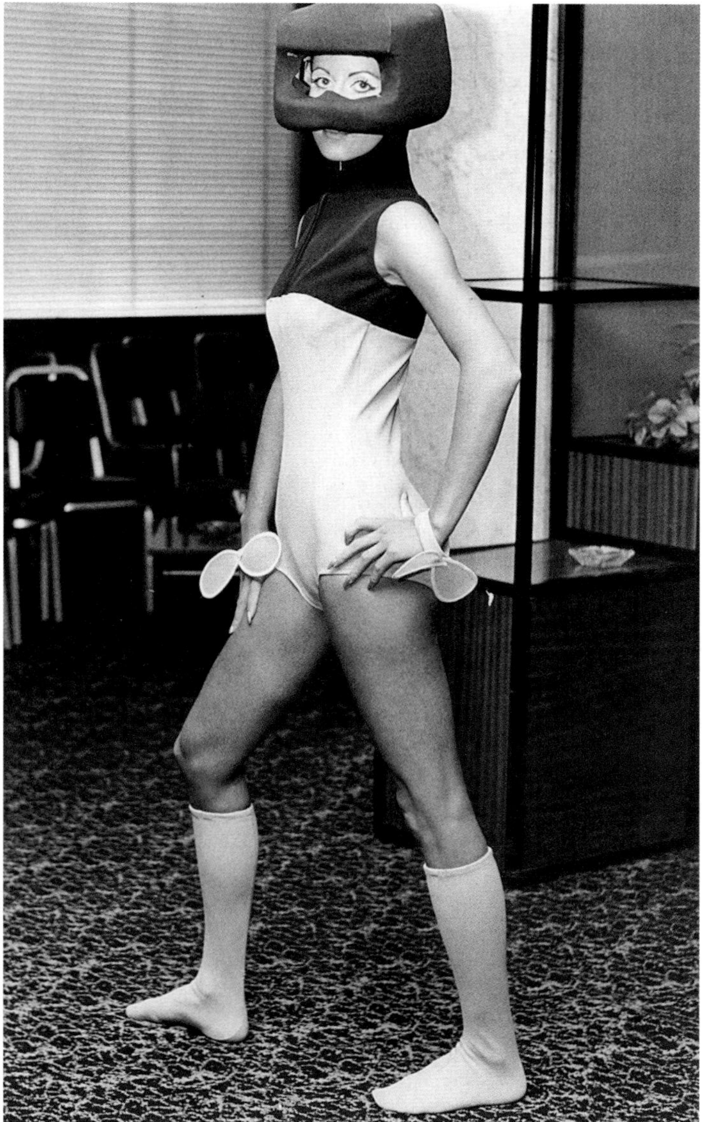

A day dress by a Milan couturier that owes much to the Op art of Bridget Riley and others, March 1966.

Vestido de día creado por un diseñador milanés muy influido por el op art de Bridget Riley y otros, marzo de 1966.

Un abito da giorno di un sarto milanese che deve molto alla Op art di Bridget Riley e altri, marzo 1966.

The Liverpudlian singer Cilla Black models a day dress, April 1966. The marriage between fashion and pop music was consummated in the Sixties.

La cantante de Liverpool Cilla Black posa con un vestido de día, abril de 1966. En los años sesenta se consumó el matrimonio entre la moda y la música pop.

La cantante di Liverpool Cilla Black indossa un abito da giorno optical, aprile 1966. Il matrimonio tra la moda e la musica pop si consumò negli anni Sessanta.

2 June 1967.
For his appearance at the West London Magistrates Court, Brian Jones of the Rolling Stones wears a boldly striped suit.

2 de junio de 1967. Brian Jones, componente de los Rolling Stones, luce unllamativo traje a rayas para acudir al Tribunal del oeste de Londres.

2 giugno 1967. Per apparire davanti ai magistrati della corte di West London Brian Jones scelse un completo a rigoni bianchi.

May 1968. Trendsetters John Lennon (left) and Paul McCartney arrive at Heathrow Airport, London.

Mayo de 1968. Ellos son los que imponen la moda. John Lennon (izquierda) y Paul McCartney, a su llegada al aeropuerto de Heathrow, Londres.

Maggio 1968. John Lennon (a sinistra) e Paul McCartney all'aeroporto di Heathrow, Londra.

A pair of photographs (above and right) taken at the Biba Boutique, Abingdon Road, London, by Stephen Archetti, July 1966. A young woman (above) concentrates while making her selection.

Un par de fotografías (superior y derecha) tomadas en Biba Boutique, en Abingdon Road, Londres, por Stephen Archetti, julio de 1966. Una joven (superior) reflexiona antes de escoger su prenda.

Due fotografie (in alto e a destra) scattate nella boutique Biba, Abingdon Road, Londra, da Stephen Archetti nel luglio 1966. Una ragazza (in alto) si concentra mentre sceglie un vestito.

A woman tries on a minidress at the same Biba Boutique.

Una mujer se prueba un minivestido en la misma Biba Boutique.

Una donna prova un miniabito nella boutique Biba.

Skirting the issue. By 1969, the mini had lost some ground to the maxi, which was deemed to be equally sexy because of what it didn't reveal...

El debate acerca de las faldas. En 1969 la mini había perdido terreno frente a la maxi, que se proclamaba igual de sexy por lo que sugería en vez de desvelar...

Corto o lungo? Nel 1969 la mini aveva perso terreno rispetto alla moda maxi, considerata altrettanto sexy poiché suggeriva anziché svelare...

...But, while the sun shone, the mini held sway. It didn't lead to a breakdown in law and order, or to rioting in the streets, though there was plenty of that about. In the end, raised hemlines led to little more than raised eyebrows.

... pero, cuando el sol brillaba, la mini recuperaba posiciones. No acabó con la ley y el orden, ni llevó a altercados callejeros, aunque fueran abundantes en la época. Al final, la moda mini sólo suscitó algunos fruncimientos de cejas en señal de desaprobación.

... ma quando splendeva il sole, la mini era la favorita. Essa non provocò né la fine dell'ordine stabilito né l'esplosione di nuove rivolte, anche se l'epoca era propizia. L'unica reazione che ormai poteva provocare la minigonna era una riprovatoria alzata di sopracciglia.

8. Youth
La juventud
Giovani

To many, the Sixties were all about beauty, and that included the beauty with which, it was claimed, drugs could fill the mind. This hippie was at a pro-drugs demonstration in Hyde Park, London, 17 July 1967.

Con frecuencia, los años sesenta se identificaron con la belleza, una belleza que, según algunos, se volvía espiritual gracias a las drogas. Esta hippy acude a una manifestación en Hyde Park a favor de la legalización de las drogas, Londres, 17 de julio de 1967.

Per molti gli anni Sessanta furono gli anni della bellezza, inclusa quella indotta dalle droghe. Una hippie a una manifestazione a favore delle droghe a Hyde Park, Londra, 17 luglio 1967.

NO
SEARCH
WITHOUT
WARRANT

8. Youth La juventud Giovani

When John Kennedy was elected President of the United States in November 1961, he was 43 years old. Most people regarded this as an incredibly young age to be in a position of such power. By the end of the Sixties, it seemed almost old, for the decade had witnessed young men and women, scarcely out of their teens, running revolutions, leading riots and challenging age-old authority.

Youth cut loose in the Sixties. They squatted in empty houses and smoked dope. They wore outrageous clothes. They listened to music that, even if it didn't emanate from the devil, was certainly played at a volume that suggested all hell had broken out. They fought. They danced. And worst of all, they grabbed the headlines…

They had plenty of heroes to choose from – Mary Quant, Twiggy, Jan Palach, Che Guevara, Mick Jagger, Malcolm X, Muhammad Ali, Bernadette Devlin, Danny the Red, Yuri Gagarin… DJs, pop stars, footballers, racing drivers, film stars, and the four lads from Liverpool.

But, as in all ages, most young people followed their peers – into boutiques and offices, on demonstrations and marches, to concerts and festivals.

And, at the end of the decade, the United States President was 57 years old.

John Kennedy tenía 43 años cuando fue elegido presidente de EE.UU. en noviembre de 1961. Mucha gente creyó que era demasiado joven para desempeñar tan alto cargo. Pero hacia finales de la década parecía incluso ya viejo, pues la época había sido testimonio de cómo hombres y mujeres jóvenes, recién salidos de la adolescencia, realizaban revoluciones, participaban en disturbios y desafiaban a la autoridad establecida.

Los jóvenes soltaron amarras en los años sesenta. Ocupaban casas vacías y fumaban marihuana. Llevaban ropas extravagantes y escuchaban música que, aunque no emanaba del mismo diablo, sonaba tan alta que parecía un estallido infernal. Luchaban. Bailaban. Y, peor aún, se apropiaban de los titulares de los periódicos... Podían escoger entre numerosos héroes: Mary Quant, Twiggy, Jan Palach, Che Guevara, Mick Jagger, Malcolm X, Muhammad Ali, Bernadette Devlin, Danny el Rojo, Yuri Gagarin... Y también entre *disc jockeys,* estrellas de música pop, futbolistas, pilotos automovilísticos, estrellas de cine y los cuatro chicos de Liverpool.

Sin embargo, como en todas las épocas, la mayoría de los jóvenes copiaba a sus congéneres y les seguía a las tiendas y a la oficina, a las manifestaciones y a las marchas, a los conciertos y a los festivales.

Hacia finales de la década, EE.UU. tenía un presidente de 57 años.

Quando John Kennedy venne eletto presidente degli Stati Uniti nel novembre 1961, aveva 43 anni e a molti era sembrato troppo giovane per una posizione così importante. Ma alla fine degli anni Sessanta, sarebbe parso quasi vecchio, giacché nel corso di questo decennio erano stati gli adolescenti a guidare le rivolte contro le autorità costituite.

I giovani furono i grandi protagonisti degli anni Sessanta. Occupavano case vuote, fumavano marijuana e indossavano vestiti eccentrici. La musica che ascoltavano non era certo diabolica, anche se suonata a un volume infernale. I giovani degli anni Sessanta lottarono, ballarono e, peggio di tutto, occuparono le prime pagine dei giornali…

Gli eroi non mancavano di certo – Mary Quant, Twiggy, Jan Palach, Che Guevara, Mick Jagger, Malcolm X, Muhammad Ali, Bernadette Devlin, Danny il Rosso, Yurij Gagarin… e i disc-jockey, le star della musica pop, i calciatori, i piloti automobilistici, le stelle del cinema e i quattro ragazzi di Liverpool.

Ma, come in tutte le epoche, la maggior parte dei giovani emulavano i loro simili e andavano dove andavano gli altri – nelle boutique e alle manifestazioni, ai concerti e alle marce.

Alla fine della decade gli Stati Uniti avevano un presidente di 57 anni.

'Let's Twist again, like we did last summer…' In 1961 Chubby Checker's monotonous dance step was all the rage.

"Let's twist again, like we did last summer..." En 1961 el monótono paso de baile de Chubby Checker causaba furor en todas partes.

"Let's Twist again, like we did last summer…" Nel 1961 il monotono ballo di Chubby Checker faceva furore.

September 1963. Australian teenagers in typical Mod clothing, including the classic Parker coat, dance the Stomp in a Sydney club.

Septiembre de 1963. Adolescentes australianos vestidos al estilo mod, incluida la clásica parca, bailan el swing en una discoteca de Sidney.

Settembre 1963. Teenager australiani con classici capi mod, come per esempio il giubbotto Parker, ballano lo swing in una discoteca di Sydney.

London, June 1962. A heavenly angel in Hell's Angel garb. The Reverend Bill Shergold (second from right) hangs out with some of his young parishoners in the Ace Café, Hackney Wick.

Londres, junio de 1962. Un ángel caído del cielo con un traje de los Hell's Angels (los ángeles del infierno). El reverendo Bill Shergold (segundo por la derecha) toma una copa con sus jóvenes parroquianos en el Ace Café, Hackney Wick.

Londra, giugno 1962. Un angelo caduto dal cielo nei panni di un Hell's Angel. Il reverendo Bill Shergold (secondo da destra) con alcuni dei suoi giovani parrocchiani all'Ace Café, Hackney Wick.

Mods parade along the seafront at Hastings, Sussex, 1964. A neat appearance and a well-polished scooter were the hallmarks of the Mod movement.

Desfile de mods a lo largo de la costa de Hastings, Sussex, 1964. Un aspecto ciudado y una escúter reluciente constituían el auténtico símbolo del movimiento mod.

Mods sul lungomare di Hastings, Sussex, 1964. Un abbigliamento curato e scooter scintillanti erano i segni di riconoscimento dei mod.

Dressed in the latest fashion, teenagers dance in a studio at the BBC Television Centre, London, during a recording of the weekly hit music programme *Top of the Pops*, 1967.

Vestidos a la última moda, los adolescentes bailan en un estudio de la BBC Television Centre, en Londres, durante una grabación del programa semanal dedicado a los éxitos musicales *Top of the Pops,* 1967.

Vestiti all'ultima moda, alcuni teenager ballano in uno studio della BBC, a Londra, durante la registrazione del programma settimanale *Top of the Pops*, 1967.

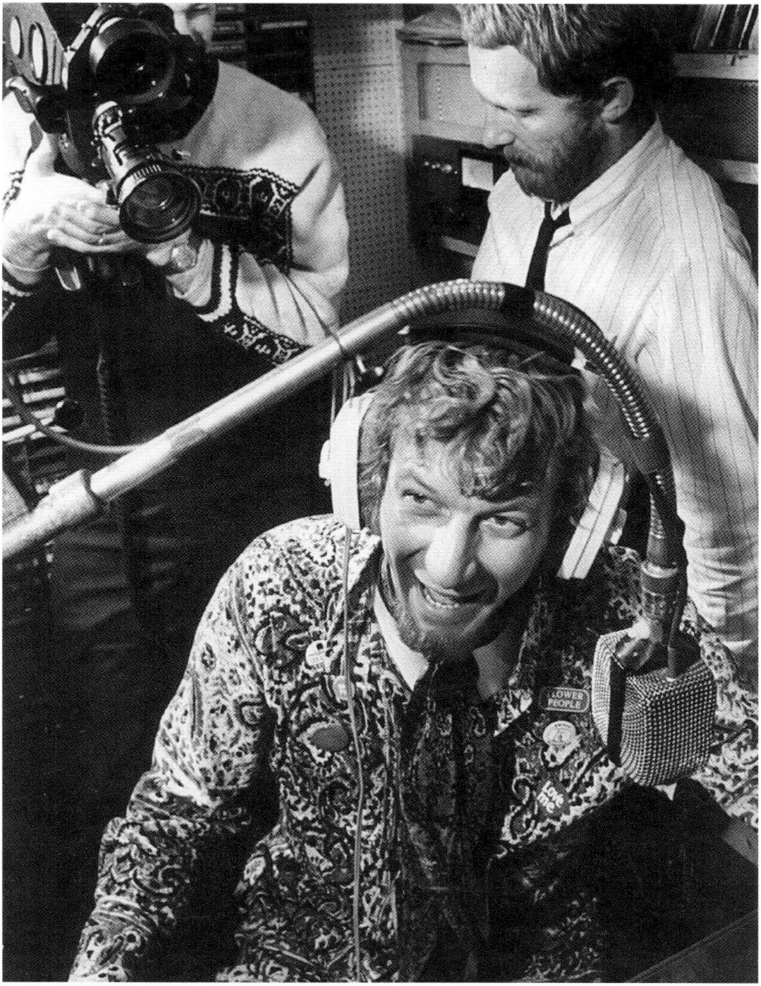

1965, off the east coast of England. A DJ on the pirate radio ship *Caroline* is being filmed for a documentary.

1965, en la costa este de Inglaterra. Filmación para un documental de un disc jockey de la radio pirata *Caroline*.

1965, al largo delle coste orientali dell'Inghilterra. Un DJ sulla nave-radio *Caroline* durante le riprese per un documentario.

August 1969. Young squatters occupy an empty building in Broad Court, near Bow Street, London. Opponents of squatting regarded it at best as trespass, highly likely to involve wanton vandalism. But most squatters looked after the property that they lived in.

Agosto de 1969. Jóvenes ocupas toman un edificio vacío en Broad Court, cerca de Bow Street, Londres. Los que desaprobaban el movimiento ocupa lo consideraban un allanamiento, susceptible de engendrar actos de vandalismo. Pero la mayoría de los ocupas cuidaban y respetaban los lugares en que vivían.

Agosto 1969. Giovani squatter occupano un edificio vuoto a Broad Court, vicino a Bow Street, a Londra. Molti consideravano gli squatter dei puri vandali, ma la maggior parte degli occupanti rispettavano i luoghi che avevano eletto a domicilio.

The outside of Broad Court on the same day. Squatters pose for Tim Graham who took both these photos.

La fachada de Broad Court aquel mismo día. Los ocupas posan para Tim Graham, que tomó ambas fotografías.

L'esterno di Broad Court lo stesso giorno. Gli squatter posano per Tim Graham, che ha scattato entrambe queste fotografie.

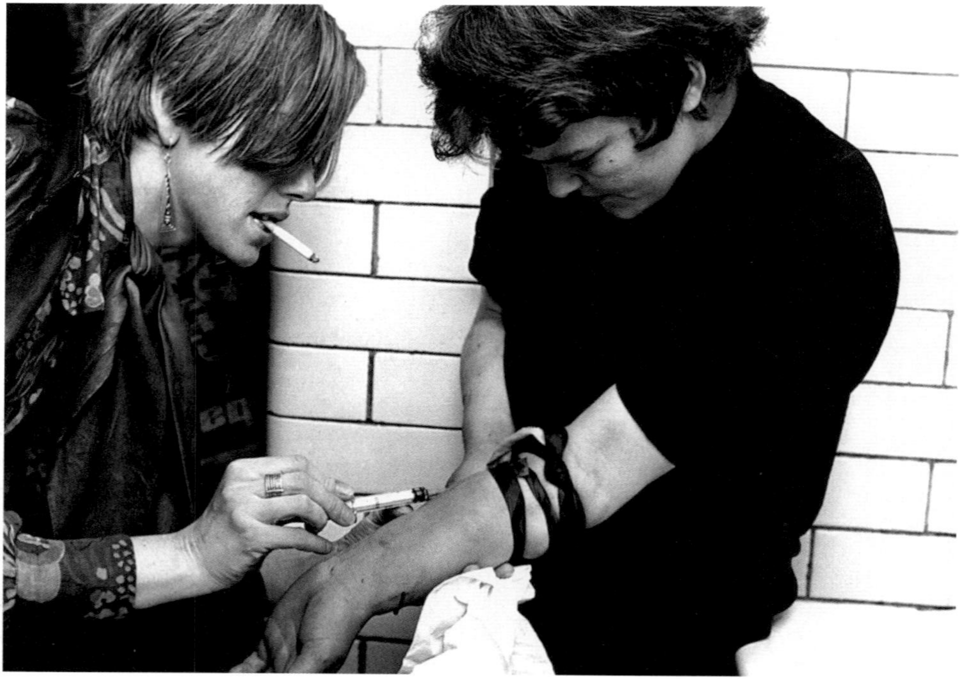

Every era has its own drugs argot. In the Sixties, this was known as 'jacking up'. Whatever the era, the setting remains much the same – a public lavatory. This sorry scene comes from 1969.

Cada época posee su argot para las drogas. En los años sesenta, a esto se le llamaba "chutarse". Pero, sea la época que sea, el escenario es casi siempre el mismo: los lavabos públicos. Esta triste escena data de 1969.

Ogni epoca ha i suoi gerghi legati alle droghe. Negli anni Sessanta si diceva "farsi una pera". Ma quale che sia l'epoca, l'ambiente resta lo stesso: un gabinetto pubblico. Questa triste scena è stata fotografata nel 1969.

All over the world, the Sixties witnessed a massive number of demonstrations to legalize the use of cannabis. Here one protestor makes his point by smoking a large reefer, 1966.

Los años sesenta fueron testigos de un gran número de manifestaciones en favor de la legalización del cannabis. En la foto, uno de los manifestantes defiende su punto de vista fumándose un larguísimo porro, 1966.

Negli anni Sessanta, in tutto il mondo si svolsero manifestazioni per legalizzare la cannabis. Qui sopra un manifestante difende il suo punto di vista fumandosi una megacanna, 1966.

A member of the Hell's Angels at the Rolling Stones Concert in memory of Brian Jones, London, 5 July 1969.

Un miembro de los Hell's Angels en el concierto que ofrecieron los Rolling Stones en memoria de Brian Jones, Londres, 5 de julio de 1969.

Un membro degli Hell's Angels al concerto dei Rolling Stones in memoria di Brian Jones, Londra, 5 luglio 1969.

Hippy heaven. Two pop fans in their finery at the Hyde Park free open-air concert, 20 September 1969.

El paraíso hippy. Dos *fans* de la música pop con sus mejores galas en un concierto gratuito al aire libre en Hyde Park, 20 de septiembre de 1969.

Il paradiso degli hippie. Due fan della musica pop, con i costumi rituali, al concerto gratuito a Hyde Park il 20 settembre 1969.

5 July 1969. Two members of the vast crowd in Hyde Park dance together during the Stones concert. Ex-Stones guitarist Brian Jones had died just two days before the concert was given.

5 de julio de 1969. Dos personas entre la multitud de Hyde Park bailan en el concierto de los Rolling Stones. El ex guitarrista de los Stones Brian Jones había muerto dos días antes de este concierto.

5 luglio 1969. Due spettatori ballano insieme durante un concerto degli Stones a Hyde Park. Il chitarrista degli Stones Brian Jones era morto due giorni prima del concerto.

A small section of the half million who came to Woodstock, near Bethel, New York, on that famous day in August 1969. The fans endured traffic jams, food and water shortages, and torrential downpours to enjoy the Festival.

Una pequeña parte del medio millón de personas que acudieron a Woodstock, cerca de Bethel, Nueva York, en aquel famoso día de agosto de 1969. Para disfrutar del festival, los *fans* tuvieron que soportar aglomeraciones, escasez de comida y agua y lluvias torrenciales.

Nell'agosto 1969 a Woodstock, vicino a Bethel, nello stato di New York, mezzo milione di persone sfidarono gli ingorghi stradali, la scarsità di cibo e acqua e la pioggia torrenziale per assistere a un Festival pop.

9. The space age
La era espacial
L'era spaziale

November 1969. A US astronaut returns to *Apollo 12* with a container of soil from the surface of the Moon. He has a camera to record his movements, and a check list on his left wrist. A fellow astronaut is reflected in his faceshield.

Noviembre de 1969. Un astronauta estadounidense regresa al *Apollo 12* con un tubo que contiene suelo de la superficie lunar. Graba sus movimientos con una cámara, y lleva una lista de comprobaciones en su muñeca izquierda. En su casco se refleja la imagen de un colega.

Novembre 1969. Un astronauta americano ritorna alla *Apollo 12* con un campione di suolo della superficie lunare. Ha una videocamera per registrare i suoi movimenti e una check-list al polso sinistro. Sulla visiera del casco si riflette un altro astronauta.

MAIN MOM
TALK

9. The space age
La era espacial
L'era spaziale

The billions of dollars and roubles that had been gobbled up in the space race of the Fifties at last returned a dividend. Man, and woman, conquered space. Millions of people round the world scanned the blurred images on television screens and the front pages of newspapers, and saw the first ever long-distance photographs of the Earth, and close-ups of the Moon.

It was a staggering achievement, accomplished for a mixture of good and bad reasons. There was a genuine scientific desire to find out more about our universe. There was also a squalid contest to see whether East or West would gain control of a tiny corner of the infinite.

The Soviet Union got into space first. A smiling Russian spaceman named Yuri Gagarin was the first human to follow monkeys, dogs and chickens into the great unknown. He returned to Earth a hero, to be succeeded throughout the decade by fellow citizens and by Americans. By the end of the Sixties human beings had left their footprints on the surface of the Moon.

It was a great leap for technology. By the time the *Apollo 12* mission reached the Moon near the end of 1969, the quality of the pictures transmitted back to Earth was breathtaking.

Los miles de millones de dólares y rublos que devoró la carrera espacial de los años cincuenta por fin daban frutos. El hombre —y la mujer— conquistó el espacio. Millones de personas en todo el mundo admiraron las borrosas imágenes a través de las pantallas de televisión y en las primeras páginas de los periódicos, y contemplaron las primeras fotografías de la Tierra tomadas desde el espacio, así como los sorprendentes primeros planos de la Luna.

Se trataba de un logro pasmoso, alcanzado gracias a razones favorables y desfavorables. Ciertamente existía un genuino deseo científico por aumentar el conocimiento acerca de nuestro universo. Pero también era real la áspera lucha librada entre el Este y el Oeste por el control de un ínfimo rincón del infinito.

La Unión Soviética fue la primera en llegar al espacio. Un sonriente astronauta ruso llamado Yuri Gagarin fue el primer hombre que siguió a monos, perros y gallinas en la exploración de lo desconocido. Regresó a la Tierra convertido en un héroe, muy pronto imitado por otros rusos y por estadounidenses a lo largo de la década. En las postrimerías de los años sesenta, los seres humanos dejarían su huella en la superficie de la Luna.

Fue un gran paso para la tecnología. Cuando la misión *Apollo 12* alcanzó la Luna, a finales de 1969, la calidad de las imágenes retransmitidas a la Tierra resultaba ya asombrosa.

I miliardi di dollari e rubli spesi nella corsa spaziale degli anni Cinquanta finirono per dare i loro frutti. L'uomo, e la donna, conquistarono lo spazio. Milioni di persone in tutto il mondo videro alla televisione o sui giornali le prime immagini un po' sfuocate della terra vista dallo spazio e i primi piani della Luna.

Questo sorprendente risultato era stato ottenuto per un insieme di buone e cattive ragioni. C'era un reale desiderio scientifico di saperne di più sul nostro universo. Ma si trattava anche di una gara tra l'Est e l'Ovest per acquistare il controllo di una piccola parte dell'infinito.

L'Unione Sovietica fu la prima a viaggiare nello spazio e Yurij Gagarin il primo cosmonauta russo a esplorare il grande ignoto, dopo le scimmie, i cani e le galline. Al ritorno sulla Terra Gagarin fu accolto come un eroe, presto imitato da altri russi e americani. Alla fine degli anni Sessanta l'uomo aveva messo piede sulla Luna.

Fu un grande passo in avanti per la tecnologia. Quando *Apollo 12* atterrò sulla Luna, alla fine del 1969, le immagini trasmesse sulla Terra fecero trattenere il fiato a milioni di telespettatori.

April 1961. 'Flight is proceeding normally.' Soviet cosmonaut Major Yuri Gagarin, who leapt into space in the 5,000 kg Sputnik *Vostok 1*.

Abril de 1961. "El vuelo se desarrolla con normalidad." Un cosmonauta soviético, el comandante Yuri Gagarin, voló al espacio a bordo del *Vostok 1*, un cohete Sputnik de 5.000 kg.

Aprile 1961. "Il volo procede normalmente." Il cosmonauta sovietico, maggiore Yurij Gagarin, il primo uomo nello spazio a bordo dello Sputnik di 5000 chili *Vostok 1*.

May 1961. 'Everything A-OK.' US Commander Alan B Shepherd Jr, second man into space by only one month.

Mayo de 1961. "Todo va perfecto." El comandante estadounidense Alan B. Shepherd júnior, el segundo hombre que voló al espacio tan sólo un mes después.

Maggio 1961. "Tutto OK". Il comandante americano Alan B Shepherd Jr secondo uomo nello spazio per solo un mese.

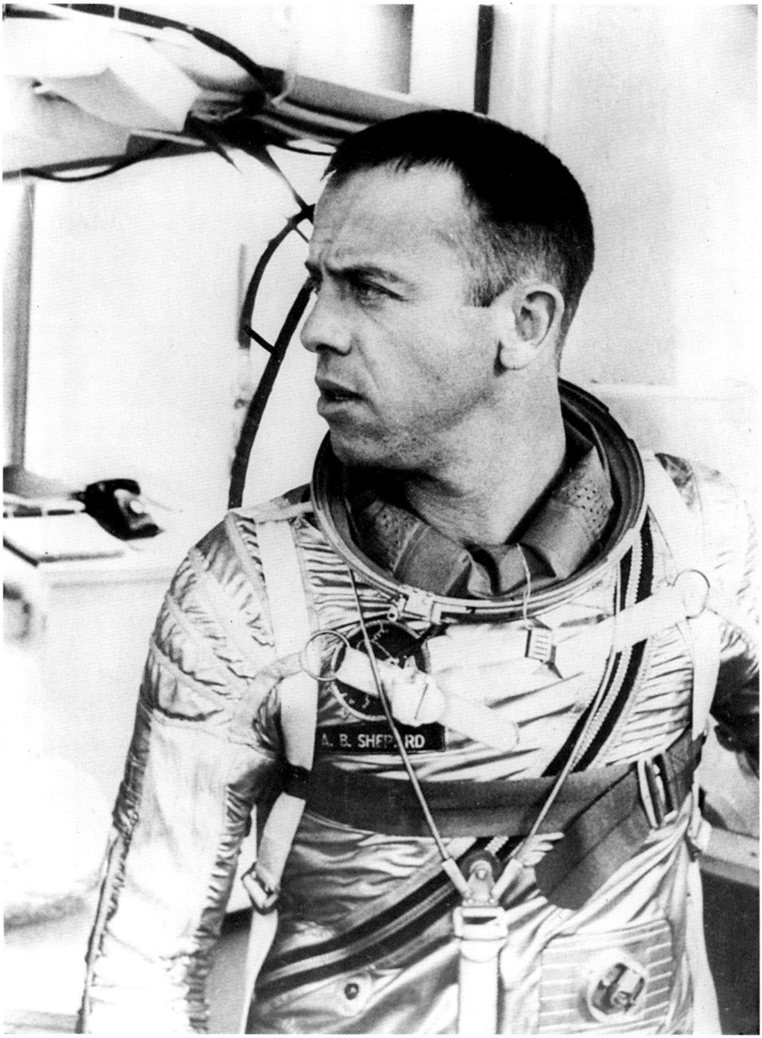

February 1962. 'Smooth and easy.' US astronaut Lieutenant Colonel John Glenn and the *Friendship* 7 space capsule in which he orbited the Earth.

Febrero de 1962. "Lento y seguro." Un astronauta estadounidense, el teniente coronel John Glenn, y la cápsula espacial *Friendship* 7, con la que viajó en órbita alrededor de la Luna.

Febbraio 1962 "Liscio come l'olio". L'astronauta americano tenente colonnello John Glenn e la capsula spaziale *Friendship* 7, nella quale orbitò attorno alla Terra.

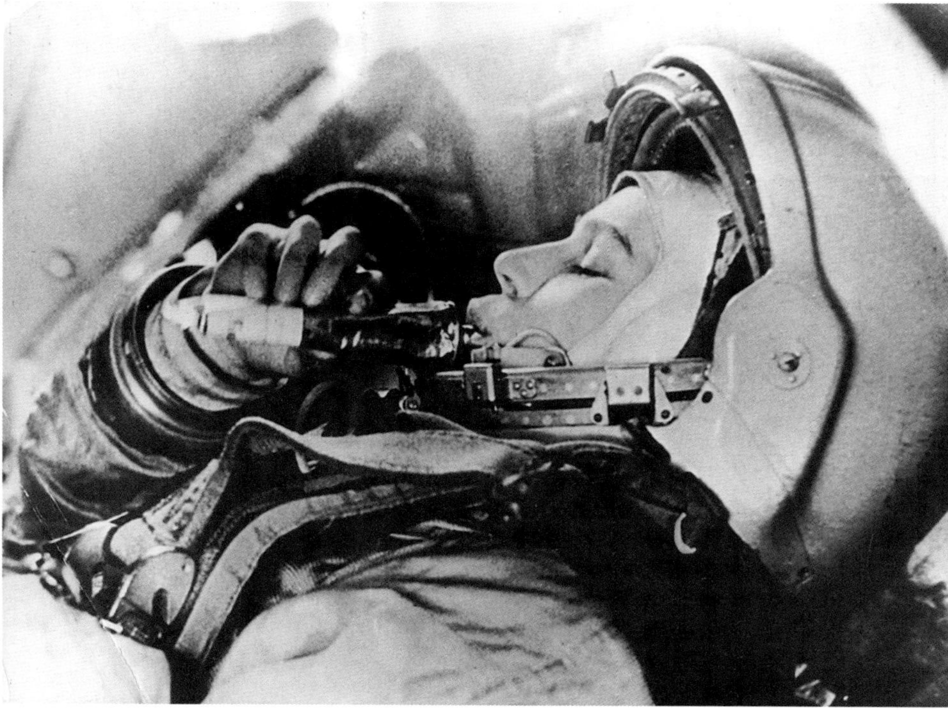

Junior Lieutenant Valentina Tereshkova, Soviet cosmonaut and the first woman in space, practises feeding in a flight simulator, June 1963. She became a great heroine and the subject of a Russian pop song: 'Valya, my love, you are higher than even the Kremlin...'

La joven teniente Valentina Tereshkova, cosmonauta soviética y la primera mujer en el espacio, ensaya un sistema de alimentación en un simulador de vuelo, junio de 1963. Se convirtió en una gran heroína y se le dedicó una canción pop rusa: "Valia, amor mío, eres incluso más grande que el Kremlin...".

Il tenente sovietico Valentina Tereshkova, prima donna nello spazio, impara a nutrirsi in un simulatore di volo, giugno 1963. La Tereshkova diventò una grande eroina e il soggetto di una canzone pop russa che diceva: "Valya, amore mio, tu sei più alta del Cremlino...".

6 March 1969. In the foreground, the *Apollo 9* command module and the lunar module *Spider*. In the background, the Earth. The photograph was taken by Russell Schweickart from the porch of the *Spider* during David R Scott's space walk on the fourth day of the mission.

6 de marzo de 1969. En primer plano, el módulo de mando del *Apollo 9* y el módulo lunar *Spider.* Al fondo, la Tierra. La fotografía fue tomada por Russell Schweickert desde la entrada del *Spider* durante el paseo espacial de David R. Scott en el cuarto día de la misión.

6 marzo 1969. In primo piano, il modulo di comando dell'*Apollo 9* e il modulo lunare *Spider*, sullo sfondo la Terra. La fotografia è stata scattata da Russell Schweickart durante la passeggiata spaziale di David R. Scott il quarto giorno della missione.

The *Apollo 9* lunar module *Spider* floats upside down in space, 17 March 1969. Inside are astronauts James McDivitt and Russell Schweickart. The module has its landing gear deployed in what was a rehearsal for the later landing on the Moon.

El módulo lunar *Spider* del *Apollo 9* flota boca abajo en el espacio, 17 de marzo de 1969. Dentro viajaban los astronautas James McDivitt y Russell Schweickart. El módulo despliega su tren de aterrizaje para ensayar el futuro alunizaje.

Il modulo lunare *Spider* dell'*Apollo 9* fluttua nello spazio a testa in giù, 17 marzo 1969. All'interno gli astronauti James McDivitt e Russell Schweickart. Il sistema di atterraggio del modulo viene sperimentato in vista del futuro atterraggio sulla Luna.

Apollo 11 clears Launch Pad 39a at the Kennedy Space Centre, 16 July 1969. The mission to put a human being on the Moon's surface was under way.

El *Apollo 11* abandona la rampa de lanzamiento 39a en el Centro Espacial Kennedy, 16 de julio de 1969. De este modo se puso en marcha la misión que llevaría al hombre a la superficie lunar.

L'*Apollo 11* lascia la piattaforma di lancio 39 al Kennedy Space Centre, 16 luglio 1969. La missione che avrebbe consentito all'uomo di mettere il piede sulla Luna era partita.

'The Eagle has landed... That's one small step for man, one giant leap for mankind.' An American astronaut walks on the Moon, 21 July 1969. Neil Armstrong reported that the surface was 'fine and powdery', and that his boots sank in 'only a small fraction of an inch'.

"El águila ha aterrizado... Éste es un pequeño paso para el hombre, pero un gran paso para la humanidad." Un astronauta estadounidense camina sobre la Luna, 21 de julio de 1969. Neil Armstrong declaró que la superficie era "fina y polvorienta", y que sus botas se hundían en "menos de un centímetro de espesor".

"L'aquila si è posata... Un piccolo passo per l'uomo, un passo gigante per l'umanità." Un astronauta americano cammina sulla Luna il 21 luglio 1969. Neil Armstrong disse che la superficie era "fine e polverosa" e che le sue scarpe affondavano "meno d'un centimetro".

Neil Armstrong stands on the Moon, some time after 11pm, 21 July 1969. It took over six hours from landing to taking the first steps.

Neil Armstrong de pie en la Luna, poco después de las 23 h, 21 de julio de 1969. Desde el aterrizaje hasta el momento en que puso el pie en la Luna transcurrieron más de seis horas.

Neil Armstrong sulla superficie della Luna intorno alle 23 del 21 luglio 1969. Gli astronauti scesero sulla Luna soltanto sei ore dopo l'atterraggio.

Richard Nixon, President of the United States, congratulates (left to right) Neil Armstrong, Michael Collins and Buzz Aldrin, on their return from the Moon, 24 July 1969. The astronauts are in a Mobile Quarantine Facility on board the USS *Hornet*, near Hawaii.

Richard Nixon, presidente de EE.UU., felicita (de izquierda a derecha) a Neil Armstrong, Michael Collins y Buzz Aldrin, a su regreso de la Luna, 24 de julio de 1969. Los astronautas permanecieron en cuarentena dentro de una cabina móvil a bordo del navío *USS Hornet,* cerca de Hawai.

Richard Nixon, presidente degli Stati Uniti, si congratula con (da sinistra a destra) Neil Armstrong, Michael Collins e Buzz Aldrin al loro ritorno dalla Luna il 24 luglio 1969. Gli astronauti furono messi in quarantena in una cabina a bordo della nave americana *Hornet*, vicino alle Hawaii.

In the last days of Kennedy's presidency, an X-15 plane is launched from a USAF B-52 bomber, 16 November 1963. The X-15 reached a record altitude of 314,750 feet (97,000 metres).

En los últimos días de la presidencia de Kennedy se lanzó un avión *X-15* desde un bombardero B-52 de las fuerzas aéreas estadounidenses, 16 de noviembre de 1963. El *X-15* alcanzó la altitud récord de 97.000 metros.

16 novembre 1963, negli ultimi giorni della presidenza Kennedy un aereo X-15 viene lanciato da un bombardiere USAF B-52. L'X-15 raggiungeva l'altitudine record di 97.000 metri.

A mock-up of the Anglo-French supersonic passenger airliner Concorde in a hangar at Filton, near Bristol, England, 25 February 1967. The plane made its maiden flight exactly one year later, and carried its first passengers in 1969.

Maqueta del Concorde anglofrancés, un avión supersónico de pasajeros, en un hangar de Filton, cerca de Bristol, Inglaterra, 25 de febrero de 1967. El avión realizó su vuelo de inauguración exactamente un año después, y transportó a sus primeros pasajeros en 1969.

Un modello dell'aereo supersonico franco-inglese Concorde in un hangar di Filton, vicino a Bristol, 25 febbraio 1967. L'aereo effettuò il suo primo volo un anno più tardi e trasportò i primi passeggeri nel 1969.

An engineer tends one of the Project Telstar communication satellites at the Bell Telephone Laboratory, New Jersey, USA, 1963. The work had to be done in a surgically clean environment.

Un ingeniero realiza la puesta a punto de uno de los satélites de comunicaciones del proyecto Telstar en el centro de telecomunicaciones espaciales Bell Telephone de Nueva Jersey, EE.UU., 1963. Las tareas debían realizarse en un medio estéril.

Un tecnico mette a punto uno dei satelliti del progetto Telstar al Bell Telephone Laboratory, New Jersey, USA, 1963. Il lavoro doveva essere eseguito in un ambiente asettico.

A Royal Air Force officer stands at the base of the 140-foot diameter Radome, Yorkshire, England, 17 September 1963. The Radome was part of Britain's early warning system against ballistic missile attack.

Un oficial de la Royal Air Force posa a los pies de la Radome de 42,67 metros de diámetro, Yorkshire, Inglaterra, 17 de septiembre de 1963. La Radome formaba parte de un sistema británico de alerta inmediata en caso de ataque con misiles balísticos.

Un ufficiale della Royal Air Force alla base del Radome di 42 metri di diametro nello Yorkshire, Inghilterra, 17 settembre 1963. Il Radome faceva parte dei primi sistemi di sicurezza britannici contro gli attacchi di missili balistici.

10. Sport
Deporte
Sport

Tommy Smith (centre) and John Carlos (right) give the Black Power salute as the American national anthem is played at the Mexico City Olympics, October 1968. They were subsequently suspended for their protest against the treatment of blacks in the United States. Peter Norman of Australia is the athlete on the left.

Tommy Smith (centro) y John Carlos (derecha), realizan el saludo del Black Power mientras suena el himno estadounidense en los Juegos Olímpicos de Ciudad de México, octubre de 1968. Más tarde fueron inhabilitados a raíz de sus protestas en contra del trato que recibían los negros en EE.UU. El atleta de la izquierda es el australiano Peter Norman.

Tommy Smith (al centro) e John Carlos (a destra) fanno il saluto delle Pantere Nere durante l'esecuzione dell'inno nazionale americano ai giochi olimpici di Città del Messico, nell'ottobre 1968. Gli atleti furono successivamente sospesi per le loro proteste contro il trattamento dei neri negli Stati Uniti. L'australiano Peter Norman è l'altro atleta a destra.

10. Sport
Deporte
Sport

Winds of change blew through the world of sport in the Sixties, especially in Britain. The All-England Tennis Club bowed to the inevitable and admitted professionals to the Wimbledon Tournament. A year later, and with matching reluctance, cricket's ruling body abolished the distinction between amateurs ('Gentlemen') and professionals ('Players').

In March 1966 the Jules Rimet Trophy (football's World Cup) was stolen while on exhibition in London. It was found a week later in a suburban garden by a small black and white mongrel named Pickles. Honour was saved, and England won the restored Cup in July – an event from which the English have yet to recover.

Boxing took many of the headlines, with a welter of high profile heavyweight fights involving a certain Cassius Clay. He began as an amateur, winning the light-heavyweight gold medal in the Olympics at Rome in 1960. Then he turned professional and by 1964, 20 fights later, he had destroyed Sonny Liston to become world heavyweight champion. In 1965 he again floored Liston, this time as Muhammad Ali.

In between all this excitement, a very young Jack Nicklaus won his first US Masters Golf Championship.

Nuevos aires soplan en el mundo de los deportes durante los años sesenta, especialmente en el Reino Unido. El All-England Tennis Club no tuvo más remedio que afrontar lo inevitable y admitir la incorporación de profesionales en el torneo de Wimbledon. Un año después, y llenos de reservas, los directivos del críquet abandonaron la distinción entre *amateurs* (*Gentlemen*) y profesionales (*Players*).

En marzo de 1966, el trofeo Jules Rimet (la Copa del Mundo de fútbol) fue robado durante su exposición en Londres. Una semana más tarde, lo halló un pequeño perro callejero blanco y negro llamado *Pickles* en un jardín de los alrededores. Con el honor a salvo, Inglaterra ganó la Copa recuperada en julio, acontecimiento del que aún no se han repuesto los ingleses.

El boxeo ocupaba habitualmente los titulares, con una serie de combates de pesos pesados de alto nivel que incluían a un tal Cassius Clay. Clay empezó como *amateur* en los Juegos Olímpicos de Roma de 1960, en los que ganó la medalla de oro del peso medio. Más tarde se convirtió en profesional y en 1964, tras 20 combates, fue proclamado campeón de los pesos pesados tras destrozar a Sonny Liston. En 1965 venció de nuevo a Liston, esta vez como Muhammad Ali.

Entre tanta exaltación, un jovencísimo Jack Nicklaus ganó su primer campeonato de golf en el US Masters.

Un vento di cambiamento soffiò nel mondo dello sport durante gli anni Sessanta, soprattutto in Gran Bretagna. La federazione del tennis All-England dovette accettare la partecipazione di professionisti ai tornei di Wimbledon. Un anno dopo, e con altrettante riserve, i responsabili del gioco del cricket abolirono la distinzione tra dilettanti ("Gentlemen") e professionisti ("Players").

Nel marzo 1966 il trofeo Jules Rimet (Coppa del Mondo di football) fu rubato a Londra, dove era esposto. Fu un cagnolino nero e bianco di nome Pickles a ritrovarlo una settimana più tardi in un giardino di periferia. L'onore era salvo e, in luglio, l'Inghilterra vinse la Coppa ritrovata, un avvenimento da cui gli inglesi non si sono ancora completamente ripresi.

La boxe occupò spesso le prime pagine dei giornali con i combattimenti di pesi massimi di altissimo livello, tra i quali un certo Cassius Clay, che nel 1960 aveva debuttato da dilettante ai giochi olimpici di Roma vincendo la medaglia d'oro dei pesi medio-leggeri. Diventato professionista, nel 1964, 20 combattimenti più tardi, conquistò il titolo di campione del mondo della categoria dei pesi massimi dopo aver messo KO Sonny Liston. Nel 1965 sconfisse di nuovo Liston, questa volta con il nome di Muhammad Ali.

Ultimo ma non meno importante, il giovanissimo campione Jack Nicklaus, che conquistò il titolo ai Masters americani di golf.

Goal! Geoff Hurst of England (foreground) scores the winning goal against Argentina in the quarter-final of the World Cup, 23 July 1966. Team mates include Roger Hunt (left, with arms raised) and Alan Ball (right).

¡Gol! Geoff Hurst, del equipo de Inglaterra (primer plano), marca el gol de la victoria contra Argentina en los cuartos de final de la Copa del Mundo, 23 de julio de 1966. Entre sus compañeros de equipo se encuentran Roger Hunt (izquierda, con los brazos en alto) y Alan Ball (derecha).

Gol! Geoff Hurst, della nazionale inglese (in primo piano), segna il gol della vittoria contro l'Argentina nei quarti di finale della Coppa del mondo, 23 luglio 1966. Tra i suoi compagni di squadra c'erano Roger Hunt (a sinistra, con le braccia in alto) e Alan Ball (a destra).

The Italian footballer Di Giacomo celebrates while playing for Internazionale against Rome, December 1962.

El futbolista italiano Di Giacomo celebra un gol en el encuentro entre su equipo, el Inter de Milán, y el Roma, diciembre de 1962.

Il calciatore italiano Di Giacomo esulta dopo aver segnato un gol per l'Inter contro la Roma, dicembre 1962.

The last minute equalizer for West Germany in the World Cup Final, Wembley, 30 July 1966. Wolfgang Weber (left) slips the ball past the England goalkeeper, Gordon Banks. Then came extra time, and England's 4:2 victory.

Empate de Alemania del Este en el último minuto durante la final de la Copa del Mundo, Wembley, 30 de julio de 1966. Wolfgang Weber (izquierda) lanza la pelota por delante del portero inglés, Gordon Banks. Inglaterra consiguió la victoria en la prórroga por cuatro a dos.

Il pareggio dell'ultimo minuto della Germania dell'Ovest alla finale della Coppa del mondo, Wembley, 30 luglio 1966. Wolfgang Weber (a sinistra) fa passare la palla sotto il naso del portiere inglese, Gordon Banks. Il risultato dopo i tempi supplementari fu di 4 a 2 per l'Inghilterra.

Wembley, 30 July 1966. England captain Bobby Moore holds the World Cup. The British press was rampant. 'If only we could see some of that ardent and united national spirit… spill over and inspire our public life,' screamed the *Daily Express*, 'then we would lick the world.'

Wembley, 30 de julio de 1966. El capitán del equipo de Inglaterra Bobby Moore sostiene la Copa del Mundo. La prensa británica se mostró implacable: "Si ese espíritu nacional tan unido y ardiente... se extendiera e inspirara nuestra vida pública —clamaba el *Daily Express*— el mundo estaría a nuestros pies".

Wembley, 30 luglio 1966. Il capitano della squadra inglese Bobby Moore regge la Coppa del mondo. La stampa britannica si scatenò: "Se soltanto un briciolo di questo ardente spirito nazionale… si riversasse nella vita pubblica", recriminò il *Daily Express*, "…allora il mondo sarebbe ai nostri piedi".

1966. Gordon Banks shows his all round goal-keeper skills by catching a stray dog which had invaded the pitch during a football match.

1966. Gordon Banks hace una demostración de su extrema habilidad como portero al atrapar a un perro extraviado que invadió el campo durante un partido.

1966. Gordon Banks dà prova delle sue versatili doti di portiere catturando un cane randagio che aveva invaso il campo durante una partita.

Eusebio (centre) is tackled from behind by Maldini during the European Cup Final between Benefica and Milan, Wembley, May 1963.

Maldini entra a Eusebio (centro) por la espalda durante la final de la Copa de Europa entre el Benfica y el Milán, Wembley, mayo de 1963.

Eusebio (al centro) viene sgambettato da dietro da Maldini durante la finale della Coppa d'Europa tra Benfica e Milan, Wembley, maggio 1963.

Russian athlete Tamara Press creates a new Olympic record of 59 feet 6 inches (18.14 metres) in the final of the Women's Shot Put, Tokyo, October 1964.

La atleta rusa Tamara Press consigue un nuevo récord olímpico con 18,14 m en la final femenina del lanzamiento de peso, Tokio, octubre de 1964.

L'atleta russa Tamara Press stabilisce il nuovo record olimpico di 18,14 metri nella finale del lancio del peso femminile, Tokyo, ottobre 1964.

Torbjorn Yggeseth of Norway glides through the air in the ski-jump event at the Winter Olympics, Innsbruck, Austria, February 1964.

El noruego Torbjorn Yggeseth se desliza por el aire durante la prueba de saltos de esquí en los Juegos Olímpicos de invierno de Innsbruck, Austria, febrero de 1964.

Il norvegese Torbjorn Yggeseth durante la sua prova di salto dal trampolino alle Olimpiadi invernali di Innsbruck, Austria, febbraio 1964.

September 1960. The winners of Olympic medals for light-heavyweight boxing line up on the podium at the stadium in Rome. Cassius Clay (centre), gold medallist; Zbigniew Pietrzykowski of Poland (right), silver; Guilio Saraudi of Italy (far left) and Anthony Madigan of Australia, joint bronze.

Septiembre de 1960. Los ganadores de medallas olímpicas de boxeo del peso medio alineados en el podio en el estadio de Roma. Cassius Clay (centro), oro; el polaco Zbigniew Pietrzyowski (derecha), plata; el italiano Guilio Saraudi (extremo izquierdo) y el australiano Anthony Madigan, que compartieron la medalla de bronce.

Settembre 1960. I vincitori della medaglia olimpica per i pesi medio-leggeri della boxe sul podio dello stadio di Roma. Cassius Clay (al centro), medaglia d'oro; il polacco Zbigniew Pietrzykowski (a destra) argento; l'italiano Giulio Saraudi (estrema sinistra) e l'australiano Anthony Madigan, bronzo.

February 1964.
After defeating Liston, Cassius Clay floats like a butterfly across the ring to urge reporters to 'eat their words'.

Febrero de 1964.
Tras derrotar a Liston, Cassius Clay corre al otro lado del ring y les grita a los periodistas que se traguen las palabras proferidas antes del combate.

Febbraio 1964.
Dopo aver sconfitto Liston, Cassius Clay saltella sul ring prendendosi gioco dei giornalisti che avevano predetto la vittoria del suo avversario.

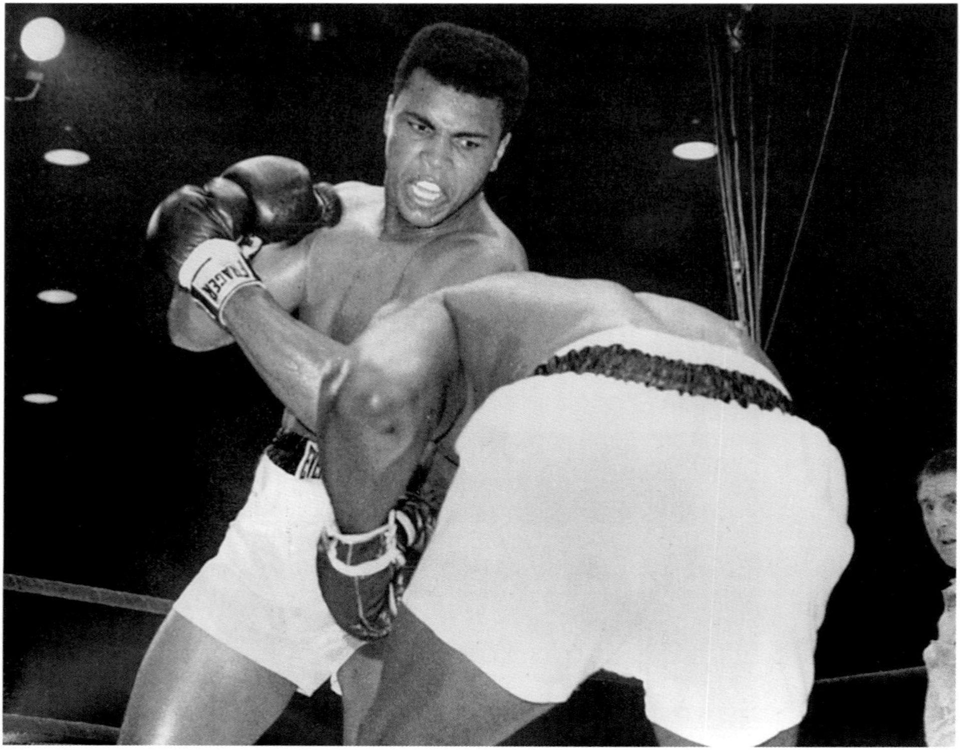

Cassius Clay in action against Sonny Liston during the Heavyweight title fight, at Miami Beach, Florida, 27 February 1964. Clay was awarded the fight when Liston failed to come out of his corner at the start of the seventh round.

Cassius Clay ataca a Sonny Liston en el combate de los pesos pesados en Miami Beach, Florida, 27 de febrero de 1964. Clay resultó campeón cuando, al comienzo del séptimo asalto, Liston no pudo levantarse de su rincón.

Cassius Clay in azione contro Sonny Liston durante il combattimento per il titolo dei pesi massimi a Miami Beach, Florida, 27 febbraio 1964. Clay si aggiudicò l'incontro quando Liston, all'inizio del settimo round, restò intrappolato nel suo angolo.

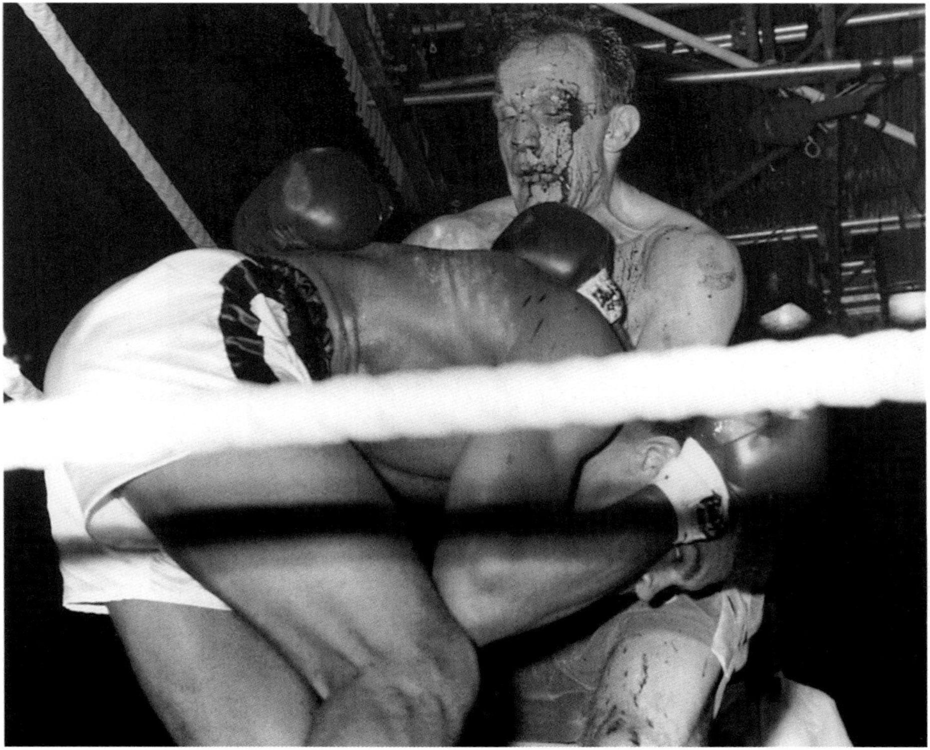

Bloodied, battered, but brave – Henry Cooper of England takes the battle to Muhammad Ali (formerly Cassius Clay) during their title fight in London, 21 May 1966.

Sangrando y magullado pero lleno de valor, el inglés Henry Cooper continúa haciendo frente a Muhammad Ali (antes Cassius Clay) durante su combate por el título de campeón del mundo en Londres, 21 de mayo de 1966.

Nonostante la spaccatura del sopracciglio che sanguina copiosamente, l'inglese Henry Cooper continua a combattere contro Muhammad Ali (ex Cassius Clay) per il titolo dei pesi massimi a Londra, 21 maggio 1966.

July 1969. American tennis player Billie Jean King in action at Wimbledon. She was champion in 1966, 1967 and 1968, but lost in 1969.

Julio de 1969. La tenista estadounidense Billie Jean King en plena acción en Wimbledon. Fue campeona en 1966, 1967 y 1968, pero perdió en 1969.

Luglio 1969. La tennista americana Billie Jean King in azione a Wimbledon. Fu campionessa nel 1966, 1967 e 1968, ma perse nel 1969.

June 1962. Rod Laver of Australia successfully defends his Wimbledon title against P Darmon.

Junio de 1962. El australiano Rod Laver defiende con éxito su título de campeón de Wimbledon ante P. Darmon.

Giugno 1962. L'australiano Rod Laver difende con successo il suo titolo di Wimbledon contro P. Darmon.

Winning by a nose… This award-winning sports photograph by Reg Lancaster captures the moment when a runner hits the tape in a novel way, 1960.

Ganador por narices... Esta imagen de Reg Lancaster, que obtuvo un premio de fotografía deportiva, capta el momento en que un jugador alcanza la meta de un modo por completo inédito, 1960.

Vincere per un naso… In questa fotografia, che ha vinto numerosi premi, il fotografo Reg Lancaster ha catturato l'istante in cui un corridore rompe in modo inedito il filo del traguardo, 1960.

White City, London, 1969. The British athlete Lynn Davies stretches out in the long jump at the Amateur Athletic Association Championships.

White City, Londres, 1969. El atleta británico Lynn Davies se estira al máximo en la prueba de salto de longitud durante el campeonato de atletismo amateur.

White City, Londra, 1969. L'atleta inglese Lynn Davies in pieno volo durante la sua prova di salto in lungo ai campionati dilettanti di atletica.

December 1967. Speed skaters in training at Davos, Switzerland for the forthcoming Winter Olympics.

Diciembre de 1967. Patinadores de velocidad en un entrenamiento en Davos, Suiza, para los próximos Juegos Olímpicos de invierno.

Dicembre 1967. Pattinatori si allenano a Davos, in Svizzera, in vista delle Olimpiadi invernali.

August 1968. Czech diver Milena Duchkova practises in Prague for the platform diving event at the Mexico City Olympics. She took a gold.

Agosto de 1968. La saltadora checoslovaca Milena Duchkova se entrena en Praga para la prueba de salto de trampolín de los Juegos Olímpicos de Ciudad de México. Obtuvo la medalla de oro.

Agosto 1968. La tuffatrice ceca Milena Duchkova si allena a Praga per i giochi olimpici di Città del Mesico, nei quali vinse la medaglia d'oro.

11. Children
Los más pequeños
Bambini

Pre-teen Twist. Chubby Checker's 1961 dance was a hit all around the world. It drew followers from everywhere, including these English schoolchildren.

Twist infantil. El baile de Chubby Checker, de 1961, fue un éxito mundial. Sedujo a gentes de todas partes, incluidas estas escolares inglesas.

Il twist a scuola. La danza inventata da Chubby Checker nel 1961 fece il giro del pianeta, trovando nuovi adepti ovunque, anche nelle scuole londinesi, come le bambine qui sopra.

11. Children
Los más pequeños
Bambini

The world acknowledged the teenager in the Sixties, but tended to forget that there were still such vulnerable creatures as children. In the United States, 10-year-old girls wore bras and make-up. In Africa, 10-year-old boys (and girls) carried rifles and drilled with hastily raised militia. In China, they marched as Red Guards and carried the *Little Red Book*. In Vietnam, 10-year-olds were lucky if they survived.

Progressives and liberals campaigned for an end to corporal punishment in schools. Dr Benjamin Spock, author of *The Common Sense Book of Baby and Child Care*, became famous to some, notorious to others, because he took a stand against the Vietnam War. The book, which sold over 30 million copies, had been written in 1946, but Spock was held responsible for the subsequent flaws in an entire generation of Sixties children.

In the West there were toys in plenty, and a rapidly proliferating number of television sets. There was also more education than ever before, and more pressure to succeed. For a while it still seemed possible that parents would get what they wanted – a better life for their children, but not until those children had grown up.

And stigma still attached to illegitimate children, or even to those with divorced parents.

Durante los años sesenta, el mundo reconoció a los adolescentes, pero olvidó que aún quedaban esas criaturas vulnerables llamadas niños. En EE.UU., las niñas de 10 años llevaban sujetador y se maquillaban. En África, los niños (y niñas) de 10 años tenían fusiles y se instruían junto a militares de fortuna. En China, los niños desfilaban con la Guardia Roja y llevaban el *Libro Rojo*. En Vietnam, los niños eran afortunados si seguían con vida a los diez años.

Los progresistas y los liberales se unieron en una campaña para condenar el castigo corporal en las escuelas. El Dr. Benjamin Spock, autor del libro *Tu hijo,* se hizo célebre por sus críticas contra la guerra de Vietnam. Se llegó a decir que aprovechó esta causa para ganarse la celebridad. El libro, del cual se vendieron 30 millones de ejemplares, se escribió en 1946, pero a Spock se le consideró responsable de los fracasos de toda la generación de los niños de los años sesenta.

En Occidente había juguetes a mansalva y proliferaban los televisores. También existían más opciones educativas que nunca, y la presión por triunfar en la escuela se intensificó. Durante esta época a los padres les parecía incluso imposible obtener lo que deseaban: una vida mejor para sus hijos, pero sin hacer de ellos unos adolescentes mimados.

Los niños ilegítimos estaban todavía estigmatizados, al igual que los hijos de padres divorciados.

Gli anni Sessanta furono contrassegnati dal riconoscimento dell'adolescente in quanto persona, ma ci si dimenticò che esistevano degli esseri ancor più vulnerabili: i bambini. Mentre negli Stati Uniti le ragazzine di dieci anni indossavano il reggiseno e si truccavano, in Africa i bambini (e le bambine) della stessa età portavano i fucili e si addestrano al fianco di soldati di fortuna. In Cina sfilavano con le Guardie rosse, brandendo il *Libretto rosso* dei pensieri del presidente Mao. Mentre in Vietnam per un bambino di dieci anni era una fortuna essere ancora vivo.

I progressisti e i liberali combatterono contro le punizioni corporali nelle scuole. Il dottor Spock, autore del manuale di pediatria più venduto nel mondo, diventò famoso per le sue critiche alla guerra del Vietnam. Alcuni affermarono che aveva approfittato di questa causa per farsi pubblicità. Il suo libro, che ha venduto oltre trenta milioni di copie, era stato scritto nel 1946, e tuttavia Spock fu ritenuto responsabile di tutti i difetti della generazione dei bambini degli anni Sessanta.

In Occidente i giocattoli non mancavano, e sempre più famiglie avevano un televisore. L'educazione era più accessibile che mai e le pressioni per un buon rendimento scolastico sempre maggiori. Fu un'epoca in cui ai genitori sembrò possibile ottenere quello che volevano – una vita migliore per i loro figli senza però farne degli adolescenti viziati.

Quanto ai figli illegittimi, erano ancora indicati a dito, come quelli dei genitori divorziati.

December 1960. The Oliver Twist of the Sixties.
A young boy tucks into his Christmas dinner at a party held for orphans and children of broken marriages.

Diciembre de 1960. El Oliver Twist de los años sesenta. Un niñito engulle su comida de Navidad en una fiesta para huérfanos e hijos de matrimonios rotos.

Dicembre 1960. L'Oliver Twist degli anni sessanta. Un ragazzino divora la cena di Natale a una festa per orfani e figli di genitori divorziati.

Two young American boys enjoy hot dogs during a baseball match, 1960. To be young (and wealthy) in the United States was definitely where it was at.

Dos jovencitos estadounidenses disfrutan de unos perritos calientes durante un partido de béisbol, 1960. EE.UU. era la tierra perfecta para ser joven (y rico).

Due ragazzini americani mangiano un hot dog durante una partita di baseball, 1970. L'ideale degli americani era quello di essere giovani (e ricchi).

A primary-school child demonstrates the 'Initial Teaching Alphabet', 1961. In Britain this phonetically based scheme was used in experiments to teach reading.

Una alumna de la escuela primaria nos muestra el "Initial Teaching Alphabet", 1961. Este método basado en la fonética se empleaba en el Reino Unido de forma experimental para enseñar a leer.

Un'alunna di prima elementare illustra l'"Alfabeto iniziale", 1961. In Gran Bretagna questo metodo fonetico era sperimentato per insegnare a leggere.

A ballroom dancing lesson at the Holmshill Secondary School at Boreham Wood, Hertfordshire, January 1960. As a social skill the importance of ballroom dancing was declining in favour of twisting, jiving, and rockin' and rollin'.

Lección de bailes de salón en la escuela secundaria de Holmshill, en Boreham Wood, Hertfordshire, enero de 1960. La importancia del baile de salón como cualidad social fue decayendo en favor del twist, el swing y el rock and roll.

Lezioni di ballo alla Holmshill Secondary School a Boreham Wood, Hertfordshire, gennaio 1960. Il valore sociale del ballo tradizionale stava scadendo a favore del twist e del rock'n roll.

All mucked up… the perennial joys of the custard-pie routine. These children, however, are covered in the remains of a sticky bun fight, January 1967.

Mugre hasta las orejas... la eterna y habitual diversión de las tartas de crema. Los niños de la foto, sin embargo, están cubiertos con las sobras de una guerra de pastelillos, enero de 1967.

Tutti inzaccherati… l'intramontabile piacere delle torte in faccia. I bambini mostrano evidenti tracce di una battaglia di torte, gennaio 1967.

All cleaned up… Allen and Neil Dockerty polish boots on the streets of Ashington, Northumberland, August 1961. They were helping to raise money for a new Boys' Brigade headquarters in London.

Brillo hasta los pies... Allen y Neil Dockerty limpian zapatos en las calles de Ashington, Northumberland, en agosto de 1961. Contribuían a reunir dinero para crear un nuevo cuartel general para un grupo infantil llamado Boy's Brigade en Londres.

Tutti lindi… Allen e Neil Dockerry puliscono scarpe nelle strade di Ashington, Northumberland, agosto 1961. I due bambini partecipavano alla raccolta di fondi per una nuova sede degli scout a Londra.

A boy dressed as a cowboy rides through Wenceslas Square, Prague, during the traditional St Matthew Fair, 25 February 1969. Six months earlier, the square had been full of Russian tanks.

Un niño vestido de vaquero cruza a lomos de un caballo la plaza Wenceslas, en Praga, durante la tradicional feria de San Mateo, 25 de febrero de 1969. Seis meses antes, la plaza había sido invadida por los carros soviéticos.

Un ragazzino in costume da cowboy cavalca in piazza Venceslao, a Praga, durante la tradizionale fiera di San Matteo, il 25 febbraio 1969. Sei mesi prima i carri armati russi avevano invaso la piazza.

In Moon-landing mode. A young would-be astronaut celebrates an historic achievement.

Vestido para viajar a la Luna. Un joven futuro astronauta celebra a su manera un acontecimiento histórico.

Moda spaziale. Un giovane aspirante astronauta celebra lo sbarco dell'uomo sulla Luna.

Crystal Palace race track, London, June 1967. The next generation of Graham Hills, Jackie Stewarts, and Nigel Mansells? Young drivers line up on the grid for the start of a pedal car Junior Grand Prix.

Carrera automovilística en Crystal Palace, Londres, junio de 1967. ¿Se trata de la nueva generación de Graham Hills, Jackie Stewarts y Nigel Mansells? Los jóvenes pilotos ocupan sus puestos en la línea de salida de la carrera de coches de pedales Grand Prix Junior.

Gara automobilistica a Crystal Palace, Londra, giugno 1967. Una nuova generazione di Graham Hills, Jackie Stewarts e Nigel Mansell? I piccoli piloti si allineano alla partenza del Gran Prix delle auto a pedali.

Without the aid of Robin, Batman (alias Adam West) helps a group of London children cross the road safely in Kensington, May 1967. The stunt was part of a road safety film.

Sin el apoyo de Robin, Batman (Adam West) ayuda a un grupo de niños londinenses a cruzar la calle de forma segura en Kensington, mayo de 1967. La escena formaba parte de un documental sobre seguridad vial.

Senza l'aiuto di Robin, Batman (alias Adam West) aiuta alcuni bambini londinesi ad attraversare la strada a Kensington, maggio 1967. La performance faceva parte di una campagna per la sicurezza stradale.

Local children from Crystal Palace, London, parade to show the number of fatal road accidents, May 1964. The parade was held as part of 'Think Ahead', the National Road Safety Campaign.

Niños de Crystal Palace, Londres, dispuestos en formación para representar el número de víctimas de accidentes de tráfico, mayo de 1964. El desfile era parte de la campaña nacional de seguridad en la carretera "Think Ahead" (más vale prevenir).

Bambini del quartiere di Crystal Palace, a Londra, formano il numero delle vittime di incidenti stradali, maggio 1964. La sfilata faceva parte della campagna per la sicurezza stradale intitolata "Pensaci prima".

30

Schoolchildren practise road safety in the playground, November 1962. The Sixties saw a vast increase in the number of vehicles on the road.

Colegiales en prácticas de seguridad vial en un patio escolar, noviembre de 1962. El número de vehículos circulantes aumentó de forma considerable en los años sesenta.

Alcuni scolari si esercitano nelle norme di sicurezza stradale nel cortile della scuola, novembre 1962. Negli anni Sessanta il numero degli autoveicoli aumentò vertiginosamente.

Patriotic headgear, 1968. A young child on her way to a party organized by the League of Pity at the Hyde Park Hotel, London.

Sombrero patriótico, 1968. Esta niñita se dispone a acudir a una fiesta organizada por la League of Pity (caridad para los pobres) en el Hyde Park Hotel, Londres.

Copricapi patriottici, 1968. Una bambina si prepara alla festa organizzata dalla League of Pity all'Hyde Park Hotel di Londra.

6 August 1962. A young boy holds the national flag at celebrations to mark the independence of Jamaica.

6 de agosto de 1962. Un pequeño sostiene la bandera nacional en las fiestas dedicadas a celebrar la independencia de Jamaica.

6 agosto 1962. Un bambino sventola la bandiera nazionale per festeggiare l'indipendenza della Giamaica.

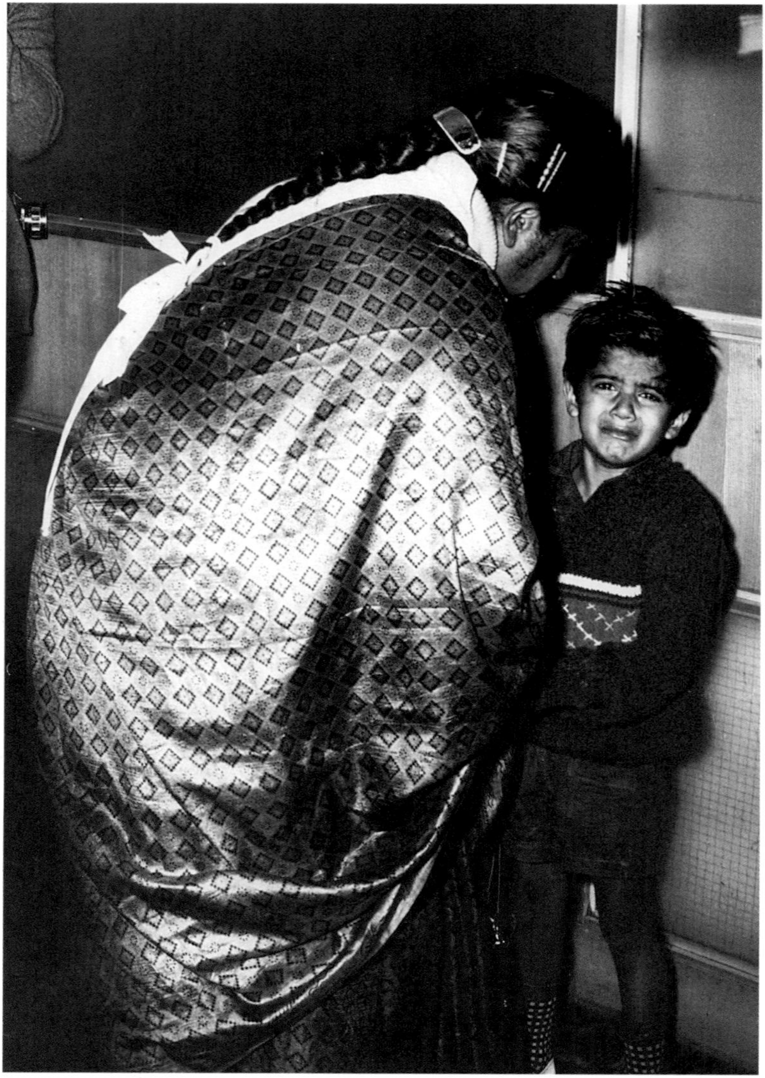

Newcomers from the East. An Asian mother and child arrive at London's Heathrow Airport, 1968.

Los nuevos visitantes de Oriente. Madre e hijo asiáticos llegan al aeropuerto de Heathrow, Londres, 1968.

Emigranti dall'Est. Una madre asiatica e suo figlio arrivano all'aeroporto di Heathrow, Londra, 1968.

Newcomers from the West. Two children arrive in Britain by boat from the Caribbean, June 1962. The steady increase in the number of immigrants was exploited by some racist British politicians.

Visitantes de Occidente. Dos niños llegan en bote desde el Caribe al Reino Unido, junio de 1962. El continuo aumento del número de inmigrantes fue explotado por algunos políticos británicos racistas.

Emigranti dall'Ovest. Due bambini sbarcano in Inghilterra provenienti dai Caraibi, giugno 1962. L'aumento degli immigrati era un argomento spesso sfruttato dai razzisti inglesi.

Chinese girls, armed with sub-machine guns, march in Peking to celebrate Youth and Vigour Day, 1960.

Jóvenes chinas, armadas con metralletas, desfilan en Pekín para celebrar el día de la juventud y el vigor, 1960.

Ragazzine cinesi, armate di fucili di legno, marciano a Pechino nella Giornata della gioventù e del vigore, 1960.

A very young Mau Mau forest fighter, 20 December 1963. The picture was taken just eight days after Kenya's independence.

Un hombrecito de la guerrilla Mau Mau, 20 de diciembre de 1963. La fotografía fue tomada tan sólo ocho días después de la independencia de Kenia.

Un giovane guerrigliero mau-mau, 20 dicembre 1963. La fotografia è stata scattata otto giorni dopo l'indipendenza del Kenya.

Joan Collins and her daughter, Tara, November 1968. Tara was rehearsing *Airs and Graces* at the Scala Theatre, London.

Joan Collins y su hija Tara, noviembre de 1968. Tara ensayaba *Airs and Graces* en el Scala Theatre, Londres.

Joan Collins e sua figlia Tara, novembre 1968. Tara stava provando *Airs and Graces* allo Scala Theatre di Londra.

December 1968. John Winston Lennon of Beatles fame, and his son Julian, in the last great decade of the fur coat. Lennon's marriage to his first wife, Cynthia, had broken up. Three months later he married Yoko Ono.

Diciembre de 1968. John Winston Lennon, el famoso Beatle, y su hijo Julian, durante la última gran década de los abrigos de pieles. Tres meses después de romper con su primera mujer, Cynthia, Lennon contrajo matrimonio con Yoko Ono.

Dicembre 1968. L'ex Beatle John Winston Lennon e il figlio Julian, nell'ultima grande decade dei giubbotti di pelliccia. Il matrimonio di Lennon con Cynthia era fallito e tre mesi dopo John sposò Yoko Ono.

June 1962. Frank Sinatra, American singer and film actor, at a home for blind children in Northwood, Middlesex, during a visit to Britain.

Junio de 1962. Frank Sinatra, el cantante y actor estadounidense, en un asilo para ciegos en Northwood, Middlesex, durante una visita al Reino Unido.

Giugno 1962. Il cantante e attore americano Frank Sinatra in un istituto per bambini ciechi a Northwood, Middlesex, durante una visita in Inghilterra.

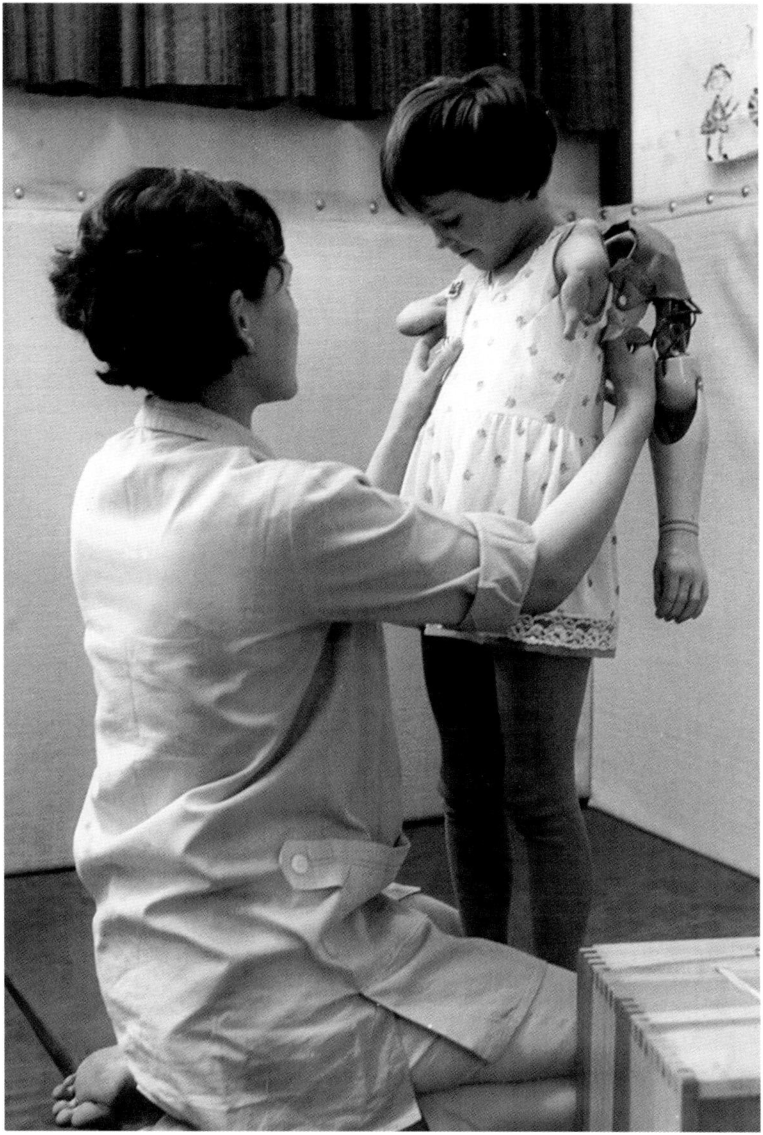

One of the hundreds of victims of the drug thalidomide, a child at a nursery in Cologne, Germany, is fitted with new arms, April 1967.

Una de los cientos de víctimas de la talidomida. La pequeña es provista de dos nuevos brazos en una guardería de Colonia, Alemania, abril de 1967.

Una delle centinaia di vittime del farmaco talidomide. Una bambina prova un nuovo paio di braccia in un ospedale di Colonia, Germania, aprile 1967.

Lady Di aged six. Diana Frances Spencer with her brother Charles, at Sandringham, July 1967.

Lady Di a la edad de seis años. Diana Frances con su hermano Charles, en Sandringham, julio de 1967.

Lady Di all'età di sei anni. Diana Frances Spencer con il fratello Charles a Sandringham, luglio 1967.

Prince Charles aged eleven. The young prince is at the Badminton Horse Trials on the Duke of Beaufort's Gloucestershire estate, April 1960.

El príncipe Carlos a los once años. El joven príncipe asistió al concurso hípico de Badminton, celebrado en las tierras del duque de Beaufort, en Gloucestershire, abril de 1960.

Il principe Carlo all'età di undici anni. Il giovane principe è alla competizione equestre di Badminton, nella tenuta del duca di Beaufort, nel Gloucestershire, aprile 1960.

12. Guilt and grief
Remordimientos y aflicciones
Colpe e rimorsi

Members of the Kennedy family at John Kennedy's funeral, 25 November 1963. (From left, back row) Senator Edward Kennedy, Jackie Kennedy and Robert Kennedy. (Foreground) Kennedy's two children – Caroline (aged 6) and John (aged 3).

Varios miembros de la familia Kennedy en el funeral de John Kennedy, 25 de noviembre de 1963. (Al fondo, por la izquierda) el senador Edward Kennedy, Jackie Kennedy y Robert Kennedy. (En primer plano) los dos hijos de Kennedy, Caroline (de seis años) y John (de tres).

I membri della famiglia Kennedy al funerale di John Kennedy, 25 novembre 1963. (Da sinistra, sullo sfondo) il senatore Edward Kennedy, Jackie Kennedy e Robert Kennedy; (in primo piano) i due figli di Kennedy – Caroline (6 anni) e John (3 anni).

12. Guilt and grief
Remordimientos y aflicciones
Colpe e rimorsi

In any decade enough harm is done by human beings, but nature also takes a killing hand. In the Sixties there were fires in California and floods in Florence. Three thousand people were killed in a landslide in Peru and there was an appalling earthquake in Skopje, Yugoslavia.

Alongside these disasters there were grim accidents. In the early Sixties hundreds were killed in a succession of plane crashes, at Orly, New York City, and Guam. In December 1963, 159 people perished in a fire on the Greek liner *Lakonia*. Astronauts Grissom, White and Clark became the first Americans to die in the space race when their *Apollo 1* spaceship exploded in January 1967. Over 300 Peruvian football fans were crushed to death in a crowd stampede in May 1964.

But the tragedies that made the biggest headlines were neither acts of nature nor accidents. There were individual assassinations, and mass killings. Richard F Speck killed eight nurses in Chicago in 1966. Charles J Whitman gunned down twelve students at the University of Texas one August afternoon in the same year. Charles Manson and followers perpetrated their massacre in 1969. The Moors Murderers, Hindley and Brady were finally arrested in 1965.

The Swinging Sixties had their dark side.

Cada década tiene su dosis de tragedias causadas por el hombre, a las que a veces contribuye también la naturaleza. Durante los años sesenta hubo repetidos incendios en California e inundaciones en Florencia. En Perú, un desprendimiento de tierras mató a tres mil personas, y un espantoso terremoto destrozó Skopje, en Yugoslavia.

A estas catástrofes se sumaron algunos siniestros horribles. A principios de la década cientos de personas murieron en varios accidentes de avión en Orly, Nueva York y Guam. En diciembre de 1963, perecieron 159 personas en un incendio en el vapor griego Lakonia. Los astronautas Grissom, White y Clark fueron los primeros estadounidenses que murieron en la carrera espacial cuando su nave Apollo 1 explotó en enero de 1967. En mayo de 1964 más de 300 seguidores peruanos de fútbol murieron aplastados a causa de una estampida de masas.

Sin embargo, las desgracias que ocuparon los grandes titulares no fueron accidentes o catástrofes naturales, sino asesinatos individuales y en masa. Richard F. Speck mató a ocho enfermeras en Chicago en 1966. Charles J. Whitman disparó contra doce estudiantes en la universidad de Texas una tarde de agosto del mismo año. Charles Manson y sus secuaces perpetraron una matanza en 1969. Los asesinos de los páramos, Hindley y Brady, fueron finalmente arrestados en 1965.

Los trepidantes sesenta tuvieron también su lado oscuro.

Ogni decade ha conosciuto le sue tragedie, causate dall'uomo o dal furore della natura. Negli anni Sessanta ci furono incendi in California e l'alluvione a Firenze. In Perù una valanga causò la morte di 3000 persone. In Jugoslavia un terremoto devastò la città di Skopje.

A queste catastrofi naturali si aggiunse una serie di tragici incidenti. All'inizio degli anni Sessanta centinaia di persone morirono in una impressionante successione di incidenti aerei, a Orly, New York e Guam. Nel dicembre 1963, 159 persone morirono nell'incendio del traghetto greco *Lakonia*. Nel gennaio 1967 l'*Apollo 1* esplose in volo e gli astronauti Grissom, White e Clark furono le prime vittime della corsa spaziale. Nel maggio del 1964 oltre 300 tifosi di calcio peruviani morirono schiacciati dalla folla.

Ma le tragedie che colpirono di più l'opinione pubblica non furono né catastrofi naturali né incidenti. Si trattò di omicidi individuali o seriali. Nel 1966 Richard F. Speck uccise otto infermiere a Chicago. Un pomeriggio d'agosto dello stesso anno Charles J. Whitman sparò a dodici studenti alla University of Texas. Charles Manson e i suoi adepti perpetrarono il loro massacro nel 1969. Gli assassini delle lande inglesi, Hindley e Brady, furono finalmente arrestati nel 1965.

Gli Swinging Sixties ebbero anche dei lati oscuri.

23 October 1966. The Aberfan disaster, South Wales. 144 people died, nearly all of them children, when a slag heap collapsed and two million tons of mine waste engulfed the Pantglas Infants and Junior School at 9.30 in the morning, as the children gathered for assembly.

23 de octubre de 1966. El desastre de Aberfan, al sur de Gales. Murieron 144 personas, en su mayoría niños, en un hundimiento del terreno. Dos millones de toneladas de residuos minerales engulleron el parvulario y la escuela primaria de Pantglas a las 9.30 h de la mañana, cuando los niños efectuaban su entrada.

23 ottobre 1966. Il disastro di Aberfan, Galles del sud. Le vittime furono 144, quasi tutti bambini. Due milioni di tonnellate di terra e carbone inghiottirono la scuola materna e primaria di Pantglas alle 9,30 del mattino, mentre i bambini erano riuniti in assemblea.

Mrs Ann Downey watches police search Saddleworth Moors for the body of her daughter Lesley, October 1965. Lesley Downey was one of the victims of Myra Hindley and Ian Brady, who became perhaps the most hated killers in British history.

La señora Ann Downey contempla la búsqueda policial en los páramos de Saddleworth para hallar el cuerpo de su hija Lesley, octubre de 1965. Lesley Downey fue una de las víctimas de Myra Hindley e Ian Brady, tal vez los asesinos más odiados de la historia del Reino Unido.

Mrs Ann Downey guarda la polizia perlustrare le brughiere di Saddleworth alla ricerca del corpo di sua figlia Leslie, ottobre 1965. Lesley Downey fu una delle vittime di Myra Hindley e Ian Brady i due serial killer forse più odiati nella storia d'Inghilterra.

Ian Brady on his way to make his first court appearance, 22 October 1965. Unlike Hindley, Brady later expressed a wish never to be released from gaol.

Ian Brady camino de su primera aparición en los tribunales, 22 de octubre de 1965. Al contrario que Hindley, Brady declaró más tarde su deseo de no salir nunca de la cárcel.

Ian Brady sull'auto che lo porta alla prima udienza in tribunale, 22 ottobre 1965. A differenza di Hindley, Brady espresse in seguito il desiderio di non uscire mai di prigione.

Tears for Marilyn. Joe DiMaggio, Monroe's second husband, weeps at her graveside, 1962.

Lágrimas por Marylin. Joe DiMaggio, el segundo marido de Monroe, llora sobre su tumba, 1962.

Lacrime per Marilyn. Joe Di Maggio, secondo marito della Monroe, piange sulla sua tomba, 1962.

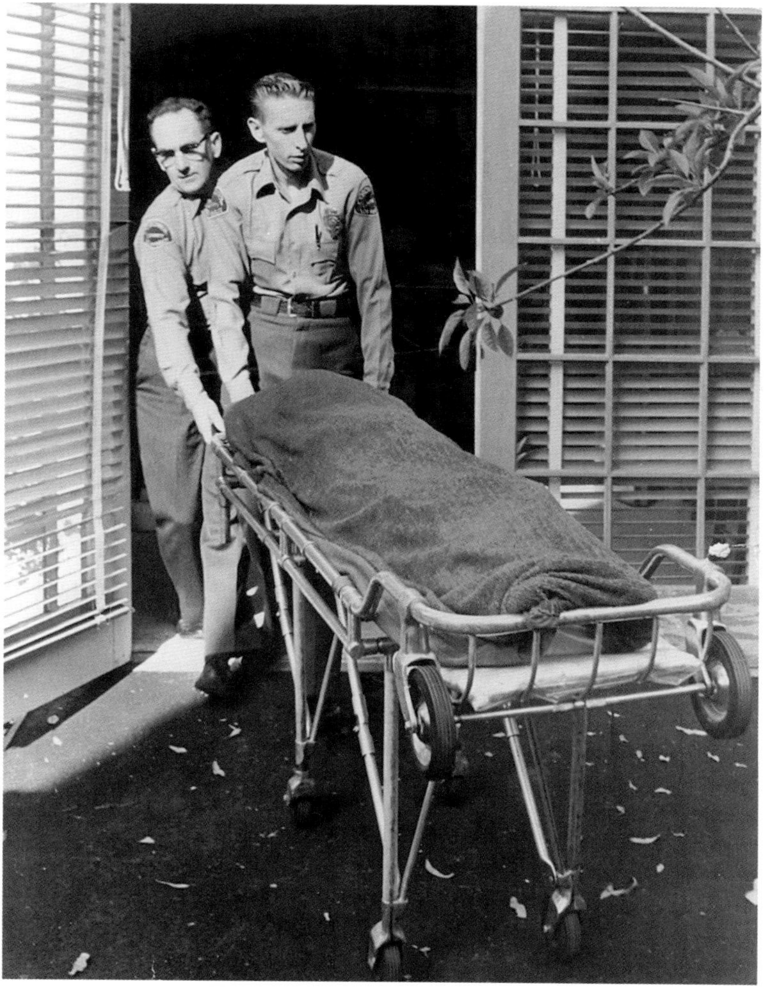

Death of a legend. Medical attendants remove the body of Marilyn Monroe from her home, 9 August 1962.

La muerte de un mito. Dos enfermeros extraen el cuerpo de Marylin Monroe de su casa, 9 de agosto de 1962.

Morte di una leggenda. Due infermieri rimuovono il cadavere di Marilyn Monroe dalla sua abitazione, 9 agosto 1962.

The end of a failing career. The wreckage of the car in which Hollywood star and sex symbol Jayne Mansfield was killed, 29 June 1967. The car collided with a lorry near New Orleans.

El fin de una carrera truncada. El accidente de coche en el que murió la estrella y sex symbol de Hollywood Jayne Mansfield, el 29 de junio de 1967. El automóvil chocó contra un camión cerca de Nueva Orleáns.

La fine di una carriera fallita. La carcassa dell'automobile nella quale ha trovato la morte Jayne Mansfield, star di Hollywood e sex symbol, 29 giugno 1967. L'auto si scontrò con un camion nei pressi di New Orleans.

'You wreck 'em, we fetch 'em'. Senator Edward Kennedy's car is recovered from the water near Chappaquiddick Island, Massachusetts, 19 July 1969. Inside is the body of Mary Jo Kopechne, who died when the car, driven by Kennedy, plunged over a bridge. Thus ended a promising career.

"Tú los hundes, nosotros los rescatamos." El coche del senador Edward Kennedy es extraído del agua, cerca de la isla de Chappaquiddick, Massachusets, 19 de julio de 1969. En su interior se hallaba el cadáver de Mary Jo Kopechne, que murió cuando el vehículo que conducía Kennedy se precipitó por un puente. Significó el fin de una prometedora carrera política.

Il recupero dell'automobile del senatore Edward Kennedy nei pressi dell'isola di Chappanquiddick, in Massachusetts, il 19 luglio 1969. All'interno c'era il corpo di Mary Jo Kopechne, morta quando l'auto, guidata da Kennedy, precipitò da un ponte. La fine di una carriera promettente.

Christine Keeler leaves court, 22 July 1963. A model and showgirl, her part in the Profumo Affair helped bring down the British Government.

Christine Keeler a su salida del tribunal, el 22 de julio de 1963. Modelo y corista, su participación en el escándalo Profumo contribuyó a la caída del gobierno británico.

Christine Keeler lascia il tribunale il 22 luglio 1963. Modella e showgirl, il suo coinvolgimento nel caso Profumo ha contribuito a far cadere il governo britannico.

July 1963. Mandy Rice-Davies (centre, right) and Christine Keeler leave the Old Bailey. It was alleged that War Minister John Profumo had shared the favours of Keeler with a Soviet naval attaché.

Julio de 1963. Mandy Rice-Davies (centro, derecha) y Christine Keeler abandonan el tribunal de audiencia (Old Bailey). El ministro de Defensa John Profumo fue acusado de compartir los favores de Keeler con un agregado cultural de la marina soviética.

Luglio 1963. Mandy Rice-Davis (al centro a destra) e Christine Keeler lasciano il tribunale dell'Old Bailey. Il ministro della Difesa John Profumo era stato accusato di condividere i favori della Keeler con un attaché navale sovietico.

August 1963. Three of the suspects in the Great Train Robbery leave Linslade Court, Buckinghamshire. The gang got away with £2.5 million when they held up the overnight Glasgow-to-London Royal Mail train.

Agosto de 1963. Tres sospechosos del Gran robo del tren a la salida del tribunal de Linslade, en Buckinghamshire. La banda había robado 2,5 millones de libras esterlinas en su atraco al tren postal nocturno que unía Londres con Glasgow.

Agosto 1963. Tre sospetti della Grande rapina al treno lasciano il tribunale di Linslade, Buckinghamshire. La banda aveva rapinato due milioni e mezzo di sterline assaltando il treno postale notturno Glasgow-Londra.

August 1966. London East End gang leaders Ronnie and Reggie Kray take tea at home. The twin brothers ran 'the Firm', specializing in protection rackets, illegal gambling and drinking clubs, and ultimately murder. They were each jailed for 30 years in 1969.

Agosto de 1966. Los líderes de una banda del East End de Londres, Ronnie y Reggie Kray toman té en su casa. Estos gemelos dirigieron "la Compañía", especializada en chantajes, salas de juego y, clubes ilegales y, más tarde, en asesinatos. Ambos fueron condenados a 30 años de cárcel en 1969.

Agosto 1966. Ronnie e Reggie Kray, capi di una gang dell'East End di Londra, bevono il tè nella loro abitazione. I due fratelli gemelli sono a capo della "Firm", società specializzata in coperture di racket, sale da gioco e club illegali, e alla fine anche in omicidi. Nel 1969 erano stati condannati entrambi a trent'anni di carcere.

The *Torrey Canyon* disaster. In March 1967 a giant oil tanker ran aground on rocks between the Scilly Isles and Land's End, Cornwall. In an attempt to prevent pollution spreading, the RAF bombed the wreck (above), before she finally sank (left) in April.

El desastre del *Torrey Canyon*. En marzo de 1967 un enorme petrolero encalló entre las islas de Scilly y Finisterre, Cornualles. Con intención de evitar que se propagara la contaminación, la RAF (fuerzas aéreas británicas) bombardeó el buque naufragado (superior), antes de que se hundiera definitivamente (izquierda) en abril.

Il disastro della *Torrey Canyon*. Nel marzo 1967 una gigantesca petroliera naufragò tra le isole di Scilly e Land's End, in Cornovaglia. Per evitare la diffusione dell'inquinamento, la RAF bombardò il relitto (in alto) prima che affondasse (a sinistra) in aprile.

Soldiers (above) in the city of Skopje, former Yogoslavia, dig for bodies in the ruins after the earthquake, August 1963. (Right) Nikita Khrushchev, Soviet premier, and Josip Tito, President of Yugoslavia, stand in front of the shattered Army Club in Skopje.

Los soldados (superior) en la ciudad de Skopje, antigua Yugoslavia, cavan en busca de cadáveres bajo las ruinas tras un terremoto, agosto de 1963. (Derecha) el primer secretario soviético Nikita Jruschov y Josip Tito, presidente de Yugoslavia, ante las ruinas del club del ejército de Skopje.

Soldati (sopra) nella città di Skopje, nell'ex Jugoslavia, cercano corpi tra le macerie dopo il terremoto dell'agosto 1963. Il premier sovietico Nikita Krusciov (a destra) e Josip Tito, presidente della Jugoslavia, di fronte alle rovine del palazzo dell'esercito di Skopje.

13. All human life
Cosas de la vida
Fatti della vita

A two-man sky taxi in flight, somewhere just over America, 4 July 1967. It was invented by W F Moore and developed by Textron's Bell Aerosystems Company, Buffalo, New York. It was intended for moon exploration.

Taxi volante de dos plazas en algún lugar de América, 4 de julio de 1967. W.F. Moore inventó este artilugio, más tarde desarrollado por la compañía Bell Aerosystems de Textron, Búffalo, Nueva York. Se concibió para la exploración lunar.

Un taxi aereo a due posti in volo nei cieli d'America il 4 luglio 1967. Originariamente destinato alla esplorazione lunare, il veicolo fu inventato da W.F. Moore e prodotto dalla Textron's Bell Aerosystems Company a Buffalo, nello stato di New York.

BELL

13. All human life
Cosas de la vida
Fatti della vita

However dramatic the happenings on the international scene in the Sixties, there was still time for ordinary people to do extraordinary things, and for the camera to be there to record them.

People invented strange contests – to see who could cram the most bodies into a telephone kiosk, to leap the widest chasm on a motorbike, to cross rivers and oceans in the strangest craft. Others sought to trick the general public in novel ways. A hoaxer named Alan Abel persuaded the American public that a topless, female string quartet would provide concertgoers with a 'purer sound'.

Researchers for the US Navy announced that the bottle-nosed dolphin had a superior brain to human beings. The US Air Force dismissed the many sightings of alleged UFOs as being probably 'astronomical' in origin. Ham, the first 'astrochimp', was rewarded with an apple after being shot 150 miles into space. Lenny Bruce, the US nightclub comedian, was charged with obscenity.

The Houston Astrodome was opened in April 1965, as the world's biggest covered arena. It was designed to be used as a baseball field. The air-conditioning was fine, but it was impossible for the fielders to spot the baseball against the background of roof panels.

Los trágicos sucesos en la escena internacional durante los años sesenta no impidieron a las personas corrientes realizar cosas extraordinarias, ni tampoco que la cámara las registrara.

La gente inventó extrañas competiciones, como, por ejemplo, quién podía amontonar a más gente en una cabina telefónica, quién franquearía el obstáculo más amplio montado en una motocicleta, quién cruzaría ríos y océanos en la más extravagante de las embarcaciones. Otros se dedicaban a buscar nuevas fórmulas para engañar a la gente. Un estafador llamado

Alan Abel logró convencer al público estadounidense de que un cuarteto de cuerda de mujeres desnudas ofrecería al auditorio un “sonido más puro”.

Los científicos de la marina estadounidense anunciaron que la inteligencia del delfín era superior a la de los seres humanos. Las fuerzas aéreas estadounidenses descartaron las numerosas observaciones de ovnis y las atribuyeron a fenómenos de origen “astronómico”.

Ham, el primer chimpancé astronauta, fue recompensado con una manzana tras haber sido lanzado a 240 km en el espacio. Lenny Bruce, el cómico estadounidense de los clubes nocturnos, fue acusado de ultrajes contra las buenas costumbres.

El astródomo de Houston se inauguró en abril de 1965 como el mayor estadio cubierto del mundo. Se concibió para la celebración de partidos de béisbol. El aire acondicionado funcionaba a la perfección, pero a los jugadores les resultaba imposible distinguir la pelota de los paneles que recubrían el techo.

Per quanto drammatici furono gli avvenimenti che scossero la scena internazionale negli anni Sessanta, ciò non impedì ad alcune persone comuni di compiere imprese eccezionali, come testimoniano le fotografie che seguono. Si inventarono i concorsi più strani – come per esempio chi riusciva a far stare più persone in una cabina telefonica, chi superava l’ostacolo più lungo in motocicletta, chi attraversava mari e oceani a bordo delle più inverosimili imbarcazioni. Altri cercarono di ingannare il pubblico in nuovi modi. Un burlone chiamato Alan Abel persuase il pubblico americano che un quartetto di corde composto da donne in topless avrebbe offerto agli ascoltatori un “suono più puro”.

Alcuni ricercatori della marina americana annunciarono che l’intelligenza dei delfini era superiore a quella degli uomini. L’aviazione americana negò i numerosi avvistamenti di UFO (oggetti volanti non identificati) e la loro pretesa origine “astronomica”. Ham, la prima scimmia spaziale, fu ricompensata con una mela per aver persorso 240 chilometri nello spazio. Lenny Bruce, il cabarettista americano, fu accusato di oltraggio al pudore.

L’Astrodome di Huston, il più grande stadio coperto del mondo, fu inaugurato nell’aprile 1965. Era stato costruito per ospitare incontri di baseball. L’aria condizionata funzionava perfettamente, ma per i giocatori era difficile distinguere la palla sullo sfondo dei pannelli che rivestivano il tetto.

October 1961.
The Goodyear Illuminated Tyre. The tyre was illuminated by a series of light bulbs inside the wheel rim.

Octubre de 1961.
La rueda iluminada de Goodyear. La iluminación del neumático se consiguió con una serie de bombillas integradas en el interior de la llanta.

Ottobre 1961.
Il pneumatico luminoso Goodyear. L'effetto era ottenuto con una serie di lampadine all'interno del cerchione.

Not as clear as hand signals… An attempt to break the record for the greatest number of people successfully crammed into a Morris Mini car, 1966.

Menos claras que las señas manuales... Intento por batir el récord del mayor número de gente que podía embutirse en un Morris Mini, 1966.

Meglio sporgere il braccio… Un tentativo di superare il record del maggior numero di persone stipate in una Morris Mini, 1966.

February 1965. Robert and Eileen Greenhill (née Pettigrew) pose for photographs outside the Church of St John the Evangelist, Notting Hill, London.

Febrero de 1965. Robert y Eileen Greenhill (nacida Pettigrew) posan a las puertas de la iglesia de San Juan Evangelista, Notting Hill, Londres.

Febbraio 1965. Robert e Eileen Greenhill (nata Pettigrew) posano per i fotografi davanti alla chiesa di S. Giovanni Evangelista a Notting Hill, Londra.

New York, 1966. A couple demonstrate the body's ability to function as an electrical conductor at a lecture sponsored by the Atomic Energy Commission.

Nueva York, 1966. Una pareja demuestra la capacidad del cuerpo humano para funcionar como conductor eléctrico en una conferencia patrocinada por la Comisión de la energía atómica.

New York, 1966. Una coppia illustra la capacità del corpo di funzionare come conduttore di elettricità a una conferenza sponsorizzata dalla Commmissione per l'energia atomica.

A handful of fun. Customers enjoy drinks at a high kitsch 'funfair house' in Munich, 1969.

Juegos de manos. Los clientes toman una copa en un bar muy *kitsch* que recuerda a una feria de atracciones, en Múnich, 1969.

Giù le mani! Alcuni felici avventori di un bar ultra-kitsch di Monaco, 1969.

Public privacy in The Bed Bar, Frankfurt's latest night-spot, January 1961.

Intimidad en público en el Bed Bar, el nuevo lugar a la última en Fráncfort, enero de 1961.

Privacy in pubblico al Bed Bar, nightclub all'ultima moda di Francoforte, gennaio 1961.

Profit from temptation. Hugh Hefner arrives at London Airport, June 1966. Hefner was editor of the *Playboy Magazine*, and owner of the string of Playboy Clubs. By the Sixties he had become a multimillionaire.

Caer en la tentación. Hugh Hefner llega al aeropuerto de Londres, junio de 1966. Hefner era el editor de la *Playboy Magazine*, y propietario de la cadena de clubes Playboy. En los años sesenta se había convertido ya en multimillonario.

Come sfruttare la bellezza. Hugh Hefner arriva all'aeroporto di Londra, giugno 1966. Hefner, editore di *Playboy Magazine* e proprietario della catena dei Playboy Clubs, negli anni Sessanta era diventato miliardario.

Prophet of forgiveness. Billy Graham shakes hands with the faithful, 1966. Graham's preaching crusades around the world are reckoned to have brought millions of people to adopt the Christian faith.

El profeta del perdón. Billy Graham estrecha las manos de los fieles, 1966. Se cree que las cruzadas del predicador Graham alrededor del mundo contribuyeron a la conversión a la fe cristiana de millones de personas.

Profeta del perdono. Billy Graham stringe le mani dei fedeli, 1966. Le crociate del predicatore Graham attraverso il mondo hanno convertito milioni di persone alla religione cristiana.

Hear no evil… Three Metropolitan Water Board inspectors use sounding sticks to listen for leaks in the water pipes beneath Rosebery Avenue, Finsbury, London, 1966. The simple device, a piece of solid ash with a beech earpiece, was better than any electronic gadget.

Nada por aquí… Tres inspectores de la Compañía de aguas metropolitana emplean sondas de madera para detectar escapes en las cañerías bajo Rosebery Avenue, Finsbury, Londres, 1966. Este sencillo instrumento, una pieza de fresno macizo con un auricular de haya, era más eficaz que cualquier artilugio electrónico.

Non sento nulla… Tre ispettori dell'acquedotto metropolitano usano sonde di legno per localizzare una perdita sotto Rosebary Avenue, Finsbury, Londra, 1966. Questo semplice strumento di legno di faggio era più efficace di qualsiasi rivelatore elettronico.

...See no evil. West Berliners peer through the newly built Berlin Wall into the Eastern Sector near Checkpoint Charlie, October 1966.

Nada por allá... Berlineses occidentales contemplan el sector oriental a través del recién construido muro de Berlín cerca del Checkpoint Charlie, octubre de 1966.

...Non vedo nulla. Berlinesi occidentali spiano attraverso il Muro nel settore Est vicino al Checkpoint Charlie, ottobre 1966.

Waiter on the water. An Austrian waiter leaves a harbourside hotel and speeds along on water skis to deliver an order, 1969.

Camarero sobre el agua. Un camarero austríaco sale de su hotel en el puerto y lleva raudo su pedido sobre esquíes náuticos, 1969.

Cameriere acquatico. Un cameriere austriaco parte a tutta velocità sugli sci d'acqua per consegnare l'ordinazione a tre clienti assetati, 1969.

Sergeant Major Tom Gledhill leaps over 20 members of the Royal Artillery on his BSA A50 twin motorcycle, March 1966. Honestly!

El sargento mayor Tom Gledhill salta sobre 20 miembros de la Real Artillería británica en su motocicleta de dos cilindros BSA A50, marzo de 1966. ¡De verdad!

Il sergente maggiore Tom Gledhill salta sopra 20 uomini dell'artiglieria reale britannica a cavallo della sua BSA A50, marzo 1966. Davvero!

The wrong man. Pressmen snap Toralf Engan of Norway (foreground) assuming he has won the Olympic ski jump event at Innsbruck, 1964. The real winner is Veikko Kankkonen of Finland (background).

El hombre equivocado. La prensa fotografía al noruego Toralf Engan (en primer plano) convencida de que es el ganador olímpico de la prueba de salto de esquí en Innsbruck, 1964. El verdadero vencedor es el finlandés Veikko Kankkonen (al fondo).

L'uomo sbagliato. I fotoreporter assediano il norvegese Toralf Engan (in primo piano) convinti che abbia vinto la medaglia d'oro del salto con gli sci ai giochi olimpici invernali di Innsbruck, 1964. Il vero vincitore è invece il finlandese Veikko Kankkonen (sullo sfondo).

November 1965.
A high speed water-skiing team demonstrate the 'flying high and dry' stunt at the Cypress Gardens, Florida, USA.

Noviembre de 1965.
Un equipo de esquiadores náuticos realiza una demostración del "vuelo alto y en seco" en los Cypress Gardens, Florida, EE.UU.

Novembre 1965.
Una squadra di acrobati dello sci d'acqua dà una dimostrazione delle propie capacità ai Cypress Gardens, in Florida, USA.

May 1963. Sixteen-year-old trainee chef Peter Maddox of Hollingsworth, Cheshire, practises fire-eating at home, as his mother and nine-month-old brother look on. The soufflé was ruined.

Mayo de 1963. El aprendiz de jefe de cocina de dieciséis años Peter Maddox, de Hollingsworth, Cheshire, ensaya un número de tragafuegos en su casa ante su madre y su hermano de nueve meses. El soufflé se le quemó.

Hollingsworth, Cheshire, maggio 1963. Peter Maddox, apprendista cuoco di sedici anni, si esercita nella difficile arte del mangiatore di fuoco sotto gli sguardi perplessi della madre e del fratellino di nove mesi. Il soufflé intanto si è bruciato.

The best of British beef. Farmer Colin Newlove rides his four-year-old Yorkshire bull through a burning hoop. The stunt took place on Newlove's farm in the village of Bugthorpe, Yorkshire, August 1963.

La mejor ternera británica. El granjero Colin Newlove cabalga sobre su toro de Yorkshire de cuatro años y atraviesa un aro de fuego. Este ejercicio acrobático se celebró en la granja de Newlove, en la aldea de Bugthorpe, Yorkshire, en agosto de 1963.

La miglior carne inglese. L'allevatore Colin Newlove cavalca il suo Yorkshire di quattro anni attraverso il cerchio di fuoco. La dimostrazione ha avuto luogo nella fattoria di Newlove, nel villaggio di Bugthorpe, Yorkshire, nell'agosto 1963.

November 1965. A good head for drinking… A man and woman enjoy a drink while they test a pair of head-massaging machines.

Noviembre de 1965. Cabezas listas para embriagarse... Un hombre y una mujer toman una copa mientras prueban sendas máquinas de masaje craneal.

Novembre 1965. Alla salute! Un uomo e una donna bevono un drink testando un prototipo di macchina per il massaggio della testa.

Taking the car for a run… The British athlete Bruce Tulloh uses a breathing hose while Dr Griffith Pugh (inside car) monitor's Tulloh's physical stress and endurance, 1966.

Dar una vuelta en coche... El atleta británico Bruce Tulloh usa un aparato respiratorio mientras el Dr. Griffith Pugh (en el coche) controla la resistencia y la fuerza física de Tulloh, 1966.

Prendere l'auto per fare una corsa… L'atleta inglese Bruce Tulloh corre con un apparecchio respiratorio mentre il dottor Griffith Pugh (all'interno dell'auto) registra la risposta del suo fisico allo sforzo, 1966.

Prince binned. Charles, Prince of Wales, in a sketch called 'Scoop', part of the Trinity College Dryden Society revue *Revolution*, Cambridge, February 1969.

El príncipe enlatado. Carlos, príncipe de Gales, en un sketch titulado "Scoop" que formaba parte del espectáculo *Revolution*, de la asociación Dryden del Trinity College, Cambridge, febrero de 1969.

Il principe nel bidone. Carlo, principe di Galles in uno sketch intitolato "Scoop", che faceva parte dello spettacolo *Revolution*, messo in scena dalla Dryden Society del Trinity College nel febbraio 1969.

Duke stunned. The Duke of Windsor (centre) and singer Jane Pickens Langley react as Floyd Patterson knocks out Ingemar Johansson to retain his world heavyweight title, Miami Beach, 14 March 1961.

El duque pasmado. La reacción del duque de Windsor (centro) y la cantante Jane Pickens Langley al ver cómo Floyd Patterson derrota a Ingemar Johansson y consigue así renovar su título de campeón de los pesos pesados, Miami Beach, 14 de marzo de 1961.

Il duca basito. Il duca di Windsor (al centro) e la cantante Jane Pickens Langley trattengono il respiro mentre Floyd Patterson mette KO Ingemar Johansson conservando il titolo di campione del mondo dei pesi massimi, Miami Beach, 14 marzo 1961.

Hand to hand… A postman stationed outside a post office in Washington, USA, collects tax returns from car drivers, April 1965. The drivers were rushing to beat the midnight deadline for submission.

De mano en mano... Un cartero recoge a la puerta de una oficina de correos de Washington, EE.UU., las declaraciones de impuestos de los automovilistas, abril de 1965. Los conductores se apresuran ante la inminente llegada de la fecha límite para entregar la documentación.

Di mano in mano… Un postino davanti a un ufficio postale di Washington, raccoglie i moduli delle tasse direttamente dalle auto, aprile 1965.
Il termine per il pagamento scadeva a mezzanotte.

Door to door… A salesman demonstrates his wares to a housewife in Bootle, Lancashire, November 1967.

De puerta en puerta... Un vendedor le muestra a un ama de casa sus mercancías en Bootle, Lancashire, noviembre de 1967.

Porta a porta… Un venditore illustra i pregi dei suoi articoli a una casalinga di Bootle, Lancashire, novembre 1967.

Odd driver... Alan Band's bizarre photograph of what appears to be a strangely shod Alsatian, 1965.

Curioso conductor... La extraña fotografía de Alan Band de lo que parece ser un raro ejemplar de perro pastor alemán, 1965.

Strani autisti... Una curiosa creatura, metà cane lupo metà uomo, fotografata da Alan Band, 1965.

Odd passenger... Captain J Edwards fastens the seatbelt on one of his pet alligators, May 1963.

Curioso pasajero... El capitán J. Edwards abrocha el cinturón de seguridad de uno de sus animales de compañía, un caimán, mayo de 1963.

Strani passeggeri... Il capitano J. Edwards allaccia la cintura di sicurezza a uno dei suoi piccoli alligatori, maggio 1963.

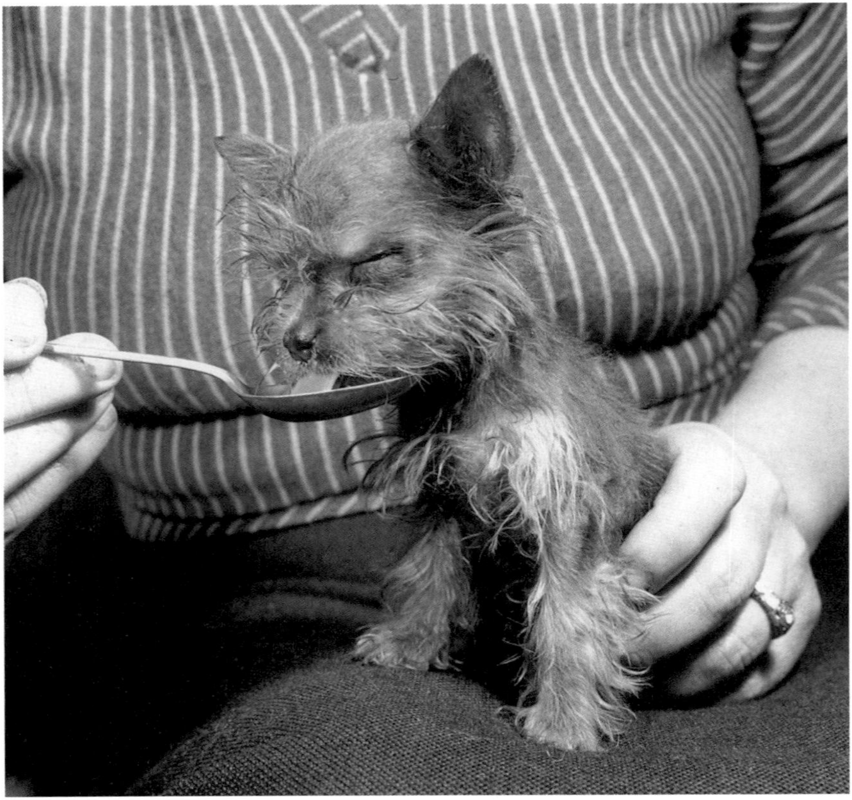

Lap dog... One of the smallest breeds in the world takes a drink from a spoon, March 1960.

Perrito faldero... Un ejemplar de una de las razas más diminutas del mundo bebe de una cuchara, marzo de 1960.

Cane da grembo... Uno dei più piccoli cani al mondo si fa una bevuta da un cucchiaio, marzo 1960.

Well-padded seat… A dog's-eye view of two chihuahuas and their owners, waiting for the judges' verdict at the Cruft's Dog Show at London's Olympia, February 1967.

Un asiento bien acolchado... Vista a la altura de los ojos de un perro de dos chihuahuas y sus dueñas, a la espera del veredicto del jurado durante el concurso para perros de Cruft en el Olimpia de Londres, febrero de 1967.

Una sedia ben riempita. Due chihuahua e le loro padrone aspettano il verdetto della giuria di un concorso canino all'Olympia di Londra, febbraio 1967.

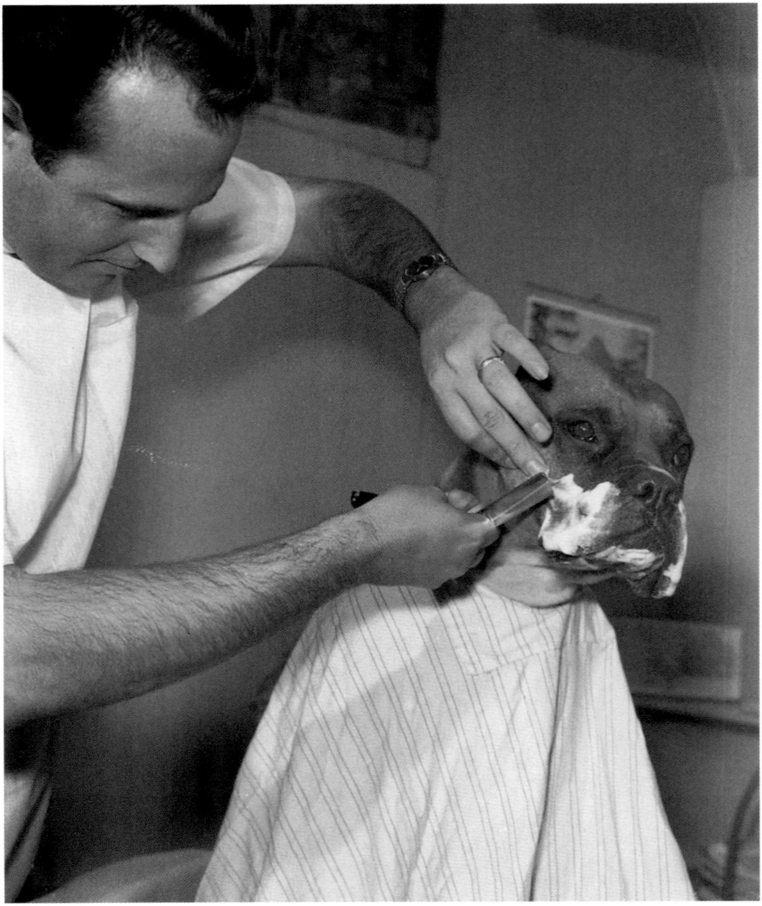

Hair loss. Fritz, a television celebrity bulldog, is shaved by a Californian barber, April 1961.

Menos pelo... Un barbero californiano afeita a Fritz, un famoso bulldog de la televisión, abril de 1961.

Baffi e basette. Il boxer Fritz, star del piccolo schermo, mentre viene rasato da un barbiere californiano, aprile 1961.

Hair gain. An Amsterdam dog models a wig made by a Dutch hairdresser, November 1962.

Más pelo… Un perro amsterdamés posa con una peluca creada por un peluquero neerlandés, noviembre de 1962.

Quel tocco in più. Un cane di razza Amsterdam presenta una parrucca creata da un coiffeur olandese, novembre 1962.

Index

How to buy or license a picture from this book

The pictures in this book are drawn from the extensive archives of The Hulton Getty Picture Collection, originally formed in 1947 as the Hulton Press Library. The Collection contains approximately 15 million images, some of which date from the earliest days of photography. It includes original material from leading press agencies – Topical Press, Keystone, Central Press, Fox Photos and General Photographic Agency as well as from *Picture Post*, the *Daily Express* and the *Evening Standard*.

Cómo adquirir copias u obtener autorización para reproducir las imágenes.

Las fotografías incluidas en esta obra forman parte del extenso archivo de "The Hulton Getty Picture Collection", reunido en 1947 con el nombre original de "the Hulton Press Library". Esta colección está integrada por unos quince millones de imágenes aproximadamente, algunas de las cuales se remontan a los primeros días de la fotografía. El archivo se compone de material original procedente de las principales agencias de prensa estadounidenses y británicas, tales como Topical Press, Keystone, Central Press, Fox Photos y General Photographic Agency, así como de otras fotografías aparecidas en publicaciones británicas como el *Picture Post*, el *Daily Express* y el *Evening Standard*.

Come comprare o noleggiare le foto di questo libro

Le foto di questo libro fanno parte del grande archivio "The Hulton Getty Picture Collection", raccolto a partire dal 1947 originariamente come "the Hulton Press Library". La collezione comprende circa quindici milioni di immagini alcune delle quali risalgono ai primissimi tempi della fotografia. L'archivio si compone di materiale originale proveniente dalle maggiori agenzie giornalistiche americane e britanniche come Topical Press, Keystone, Central Press, Fox Photos e General Photographic Agency e di altre immagini apparse sulle pubblicazioni britanniche *Picture Post*, *Daily Express* ed *Evening Standard*.

Picture Licensing Information

To license the pictures listed below please call Getty Images **+ 44 171 266 2662** or email **info@getty-images.com** your picture selection with the page/reference numbers.

Hulton Getty Online

All of the pictures listed below and countless others are available via Hulton Getty Online at: **http://www.hultongetty.com**

Buying a print

For details of how to purchase exhibition-quality prints call The Hulton Getty Picture Gallery **+ 44 171 376 4525** (fax) **+44 171 376 4524** **hulton.gallery@getty-images.com**

Información sobre licencias

Puede solicitar la licencia de las fotos que se relacionan a continuación a través del teléfono **00 44 171 266 2662,** o un mensaje de correo electrónico a la dirección **info@getty-images.com**. Indique los números de referencia y de página de las imágenes que desea.

Hulton Getty Online

Puede encontrar estas imágenes y otras muchas en la *web* de la Hulton Getty Online: **http://www.hultongetty.com**

Adquisición de copias

Para obtener más infomación acerca de cómo adquirir reproducciones para exposiciones, póngase en contacto con The Hulton Getty Picture Gallery, a través del teléfono **00 44 171 376 4525.** (fax) **+44 171 376 4524** **hulton.gallery@getty-images.com**

Informazioni per il noleggio

Per noleggiare le immagini elencate in basso telefonare allo **00 44 171 266 2662,** o inviare un e-mail all'indirizzo **info@getty-images.com,** indicando l'immagine scelta e il numero di pagina di riferimento.

Hulton Getty Online

Tutte le immagini elencate di seguito e molte altre sono disponibili via Hulton Getty Online all'indirizzo: **http://www.hultongetty.com**

Per ottenere gli originali

Per ulteriori informazioni su come acquisire le riproduzioni per le esposizioni contattare The Hulton Getty Picture Gallery, al numero di telefono **00 44 171 376 4525.** (fax) **+44 171 376 4524** **hulton.gallery@getty-images.com**

Page/reference number	Description
CTW	*Just a Kiss* (Cover)
2TW	Woman in doorway (Frontispiece)
	Chapter 1
13TW	Adolf Hitler
14TW	Hitler (top left)
14TW	Hitler (top right)
14TW	Hitler (bottom right)
14TW	Hitler (bottom left)
15TW	Hitler (both fists clenched)
18TW	Banknote building blocks
19TW	Banknote wallpaper
20TW	Sabotaging a locomotive
21TW	Dismantling a tank
22TW	Tanks into tractors
23TW	Wooden propellers
24TW	Hitler, Landsberg gaol
25TW	Briand, Foch and Lloyd George
26TW	Lloyd George with daughter
27TW	Aristide Briand
28TW	Ludendorff and Hitler
29TW	Hirohito and Edward
30TW	Mussolini, March on Rome
31TW	Hitler, Munich Putsch
32TW	Nazi oath of allegiance
34TW	Mussolini on horse
35TW	Cyclists' salute
36TW	Fascist wedding
37TW	Identity cards
38TW	Lenin in a wheelchair
39TW	Leon Trotsky
40TW	Stalin on the street
41TW	Stalin lighting pipe
42TW	Two petitioners
43TW	Starving child
44TW	Sportswomen marching
45TW	Communist salute
46TW	Citizens of Vladivostok
47TW	British communists
48TW	French troops, Ruhr
49TW	IRA patrol
50TW	Victory celebration, Smyrna
51TW	Mustafa Kemal Atatürk
52TW	Gandhi at home
53TW	Tata Iron Works
54TW	Ku Klux Klan victim
55TW	Blazing cross
	Chapter 2
57TW	'Toffs' on car roof
60TW	George V and beggar
62TW	Slum family, Bethnal Green
63TW	Dr Barnardo's visit
64TW	Disused prison housing
65TW	Athens opera house
66TW	Woking pigsty
68TW	Daily Bread Institute
69TW	A New York mission
70TW	Gentry watch farm workers

72TW Balancing books
73TW Monocle Club
74TW Huntsmen in Oxford Street
75TW Sheep along Piccadilly
76TW *White Heather*
78TW Barrel bath
79TW Mountbatten and Edward
80TW Jellied eels
81TW Free milk
82TW C C Hopkins' poultry shop
83TW Turkeys hanging in bar
84TW Fruit vending machine
85TW Coventry café
86TW Naval cadets
87TW J M Barrie
88TW Parrot at wedding
89TW Children's wedding game

Chapter 3

91TW Installing tramlines
94TW Car assembly line
96TW Opel works
98TW Dried fig factory
99TW Jacob's biscuit factory
100TW Flower packers
101TW Maize harvest
102TW Scaling Albert Bridge
103TW Glass roof, Crystal Palace
104TW Brooklyn Bridge
105TW Rooftop lunch break
106TW Underground tunnel
107TW Salt mine
108TW Bed springs
109TW Macaroni machine
110TW Telephone dials
111TW Woman taxi driver
112TW Christmas decorations
113TW *Pretty Polly*
114TW Volunteer track workers
115TW Pouring tea
116TW Roller-skating commuter
117TW Student Volunteers
118TW Strike pay
119TW Issuing truncheons
120TW Birmingham policeman
121TW Yorkshire policeman
122TW Police holding back crowds
124TW Policeman escorting children
125TW Policewoman chasing children
126TW Gendarme
127TW Pistol-shooting competition
128TW Guarding vault
129TW Training exercise
130TW Fire fighter
131TW Commandant Mary P Allen
132TW Fire float
133TW Fire at Madame Tussaud's
134TW Mrs Nelsong, chimney sweep
135TW Annie Clubb, blacksmith
136TW Ex-servicemen hawkers
137TW Toy seller
138TW 'Imperfectly Packed Parcels'

Chapter 4

141TW Helter-skelter
144TW Naked boys leaping
146TW Leapfrogging on the beach
147TW Beach fun, Isle of Wight
148TW Playing cards on ice
149TW 'Skreenette'
150TW Brighton Pier
152TW Paddling, Hastings
153TW Paddling, Clacton
154TW Diving
156TW MGM girls
157TW Pelota
158TW Novelty night
159TW Swimmers smoking
160TW Arding and Hobbs
161TW Flying-boat ride
162TW Relaxing at Brooklands
163TW Merry-go-round
164TW Skiers smoking
165TW Huntswomen

Chapter 5

167TW Charleston collage
170TW Clara Bow
171TW Louise Brooks
172TW Pavlova and Pickford
173TW The Astaires
174TW James Cagney
175TW Daniels and Lyon
176TW Greta Garbo
177TW Marlene Dietrich
178TW Harry Langdon
180TW *The Thrill*
181TW Walt Disney
182TW Cooper and Mayer
183TW Lillian Gish
184TW Charlie Chaplin
185TW Buster Keaton
186TW Keystone Kops
187TW Harold Lloyd
188TW Erich Von Stroheim
189TW Douglas Fairbanks
190TW Gwen Lee
191TW Camera on train
192TW Noel Coward
193TW Ivor Novello
194TW Percival Mackey's Band
196TW Paul Robeson
197TW The Five Aces
198TW Josephine Baker
199TW Folies Bergère
200TW Sketching chorus girls
201TW Tiller Girls
202TW Alfred Jackson Dancing Girls
204TW Weight check
205TW Dressing room
206TW Charleston with monkey
207TW Indian dancer
208TW Isadora Duncan followers
209TW Marion Morgan dancers
210TW Lake dancing
211TW Star pose
212TW 'Kickaboo' in three steps
213TW *Just a Kiss*
214TW Crossword dance
215TW Charleston in six steps
216TW Black Bottom
217TW Dancing in the snow
218TW Luisa Tetrazzini
219TW Teddy Brown

Chapter 6

221TW Santa Proud fashions
224TW Ladies model gaiters
226TW Palm Beach fashions
227TW Joan Crawford
228TW Barbara Cartland
229TW Camisole, 1927
230TW Ninette de Valois
231TW Martha Graham
232TW Dolly Sisters
233TW Dodge Twins
234TW Carrying boaters
235TW Retrieving handkerchiefs
236TW Dolcis shoe shop
238TW Durasil stockings slogan
239TW Lizard-trimmed shoes
240TW Bachelors smoking
241TW Bathing girls smoking
242TW Artificial Silk Exhibition
243TW Males model outdoor clothes
244TW Permanent wave
245TW Three perms
246TW Vibro-Slim
247TW Woman in smoking suit
248TW *Homeric* gym
249TW Mechanical horse
250TW Jacob Epstein
252TW *Le Train Bleu*, ballet
253TW Cecil Beaton
254TW *Le Pas d'Acier*, ballet
255TW Anna Pavlova
256TW Art Deco stairway
258TW Futuristic church, Ulm
259TW Strand Palace Hotel

Chapter 7

261TW Giant camera
264TW Dental lamp
265TW Steel splinters
266TW Triplex Safety Glass
267TW Asthma relief machine
268TW Spraying bus
269TW Anti-influenza masks
270TW 'Tut fever'

Acknowledgements
Agradecimientos
Ringraziamenti

Slava Katamidze 22, 38, 40, 42, 44, 46

Pictures from other sources
Fotografías de otras fuentes
Fotografie da altre fonti

Robert Hunt Library
Frontispiece, 102, 353

Topham Picturepoint
28, 31, 165, 167, 253, 291